For Dad

Disclaimer

This book contains some material that will require the use of an organ located in the upper portion of your body.

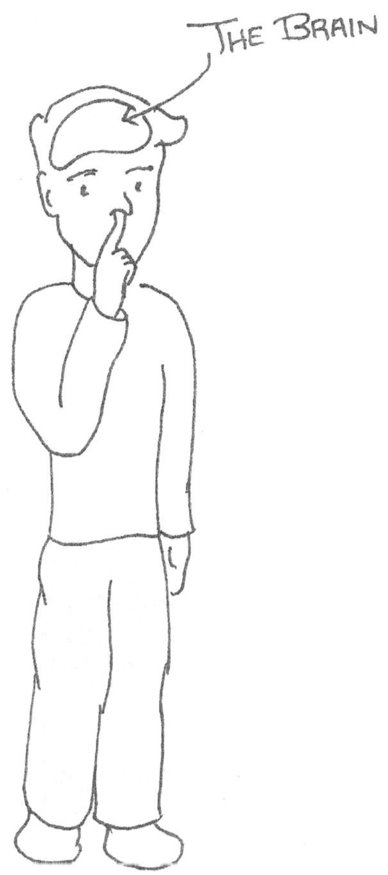

PART 1
About The Author

Take a moment, stop what you're doing, and ask yourself, how the hell did I get here?

Aside from being forgetful, I'm finding that the older I get, the grumpier I've become.

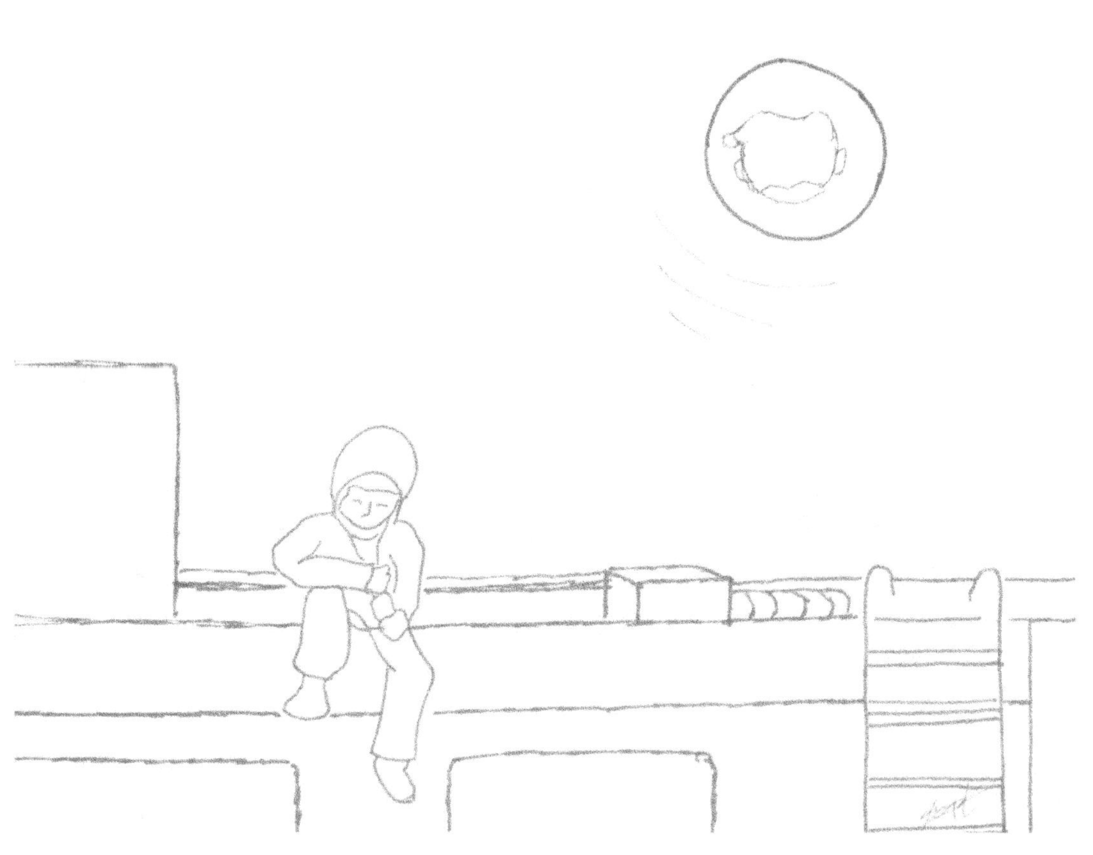

“With My Thoughts”

My journey into adulthood began when I first uttered the words, are you f*@#ing kidding me?!

To counteract my frustration with an ever-dwindling level of common sense that plagues society, I began to doodle until I no longer felt the urge to flip my lid.

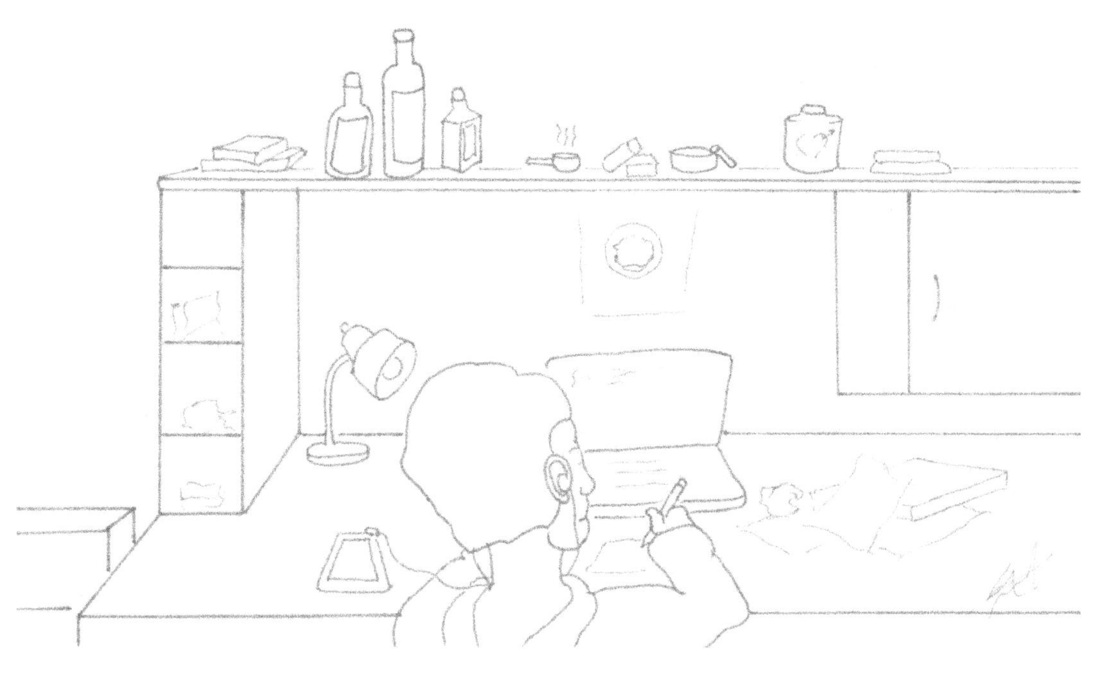

"Anywhere But Here"

The more I doodled the more tranquility I found, and soon, cartoons became my saving grace from the continuous barrage of ignorance that I encountered on a daily basis.

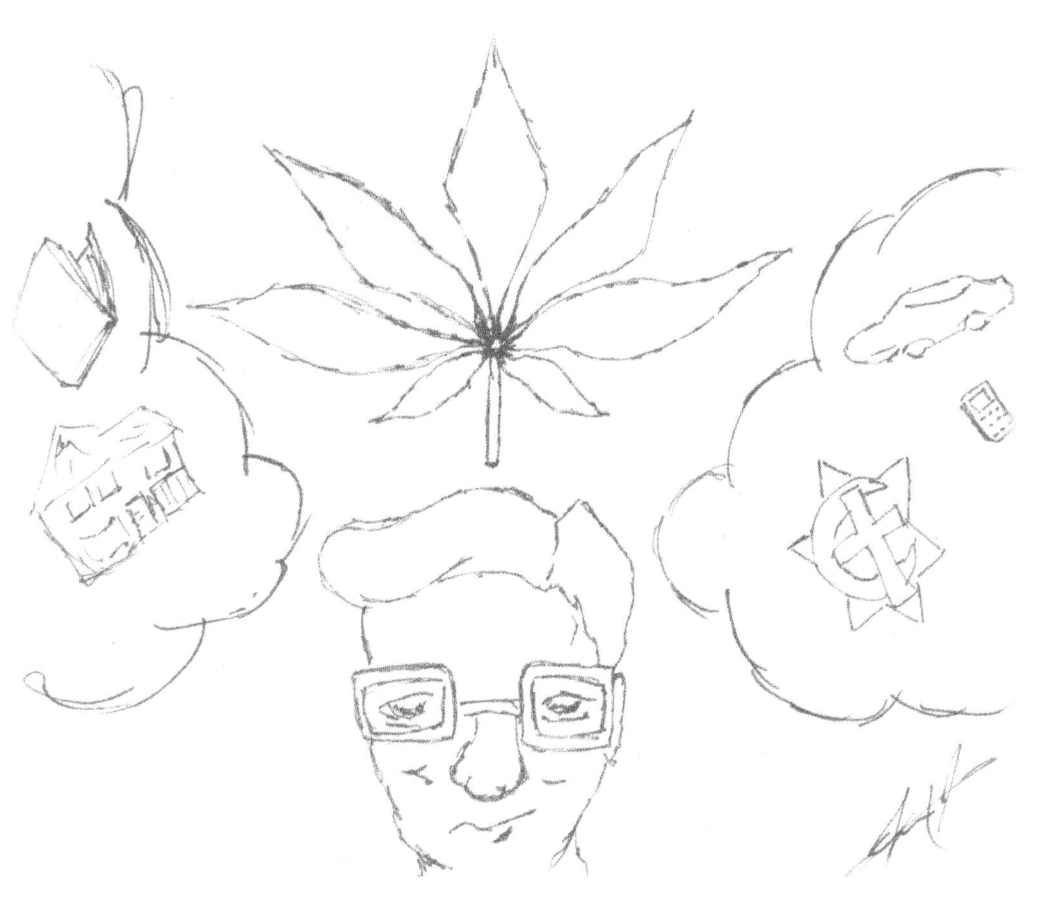

"A Moment of Peace"

Like many naive millennials, I saw an opportunity to twist my self-loathing into a means of gaining popularity and superficial satisfaction. I attempted to make my mark in the world of art and literature by submitting my unsolicited work to publishers and magazines.

I quickly learned that it's not about what you can do, but who you know.

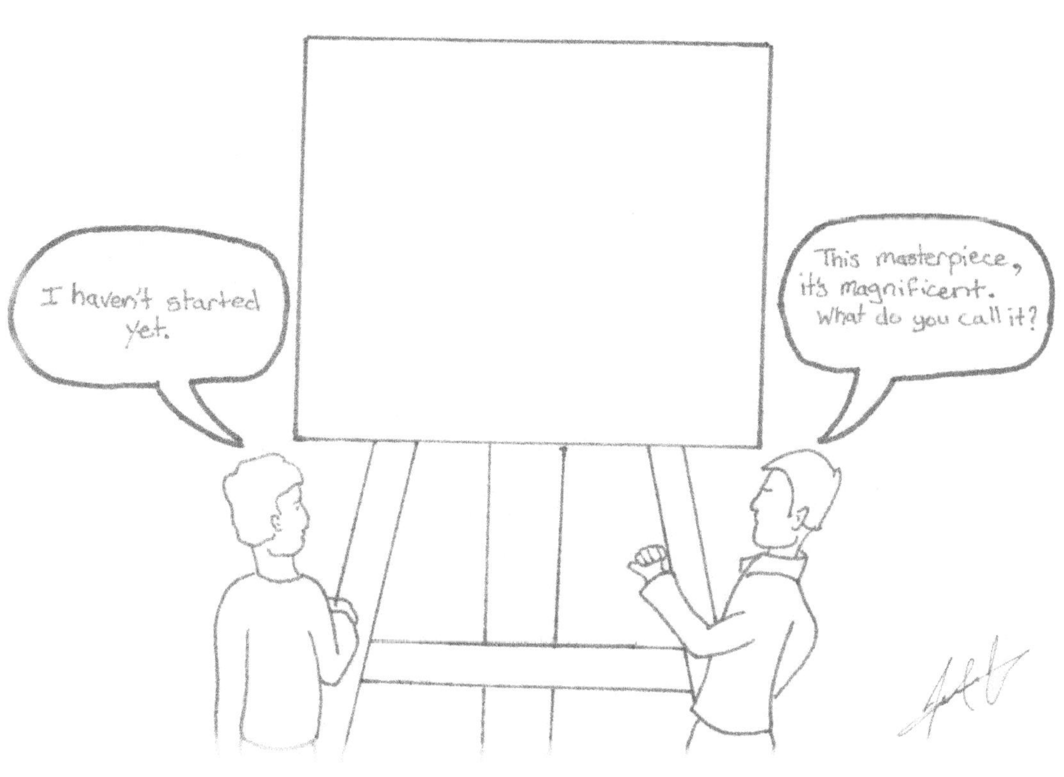
I haven't started yet.
This masterpiece, it's magnificent. What do you call it?

"Le Art"

Before I knew it, my exponentially expanding collection of illustrations were left to pile up on the corner of my desk because it was time for me to look for a real job.

Like my father, and his father before him, I subsequently internalized my anger and instead of venting my distaste towards the new social norms, I started muttering under my breath just like a grumpy old man.

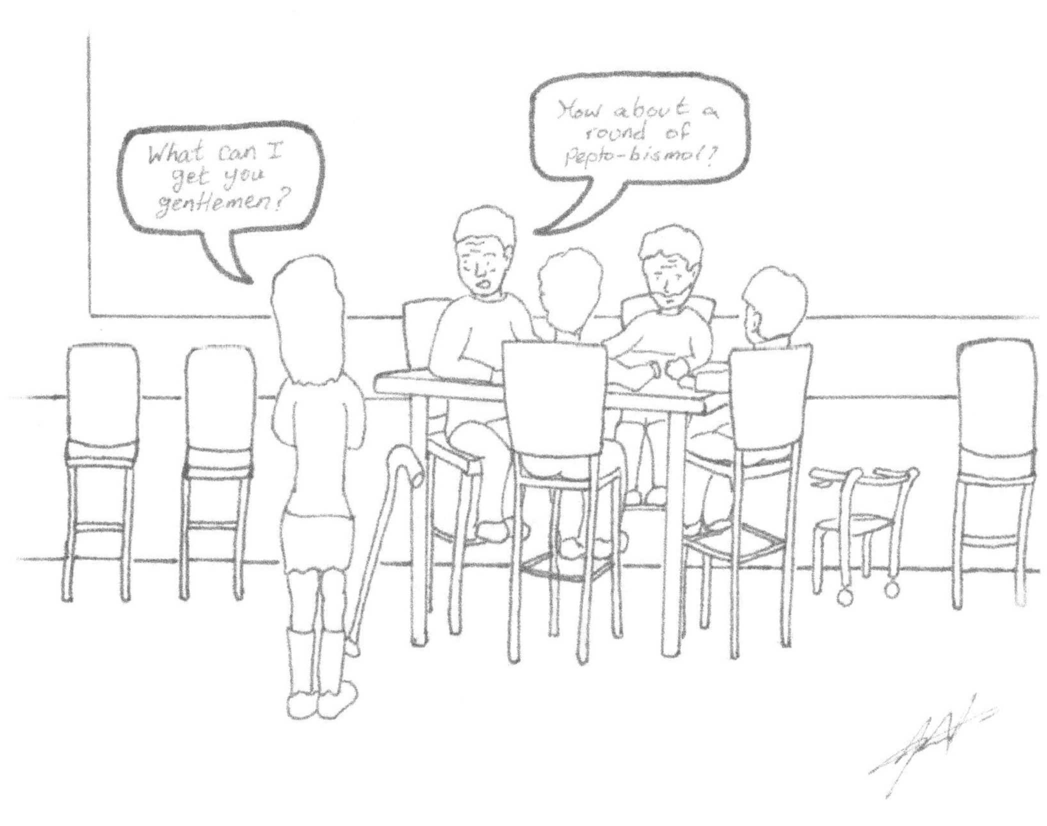

"But The Party Is Just Getting Started"

PART 2

I Don't Belong In This Century

There are a few things in this world that I know I can never wrap my head around. For example, quantum theory, or why my girlfriend is always late.

The following are some of the things that seem to blow common sense right out of the water.

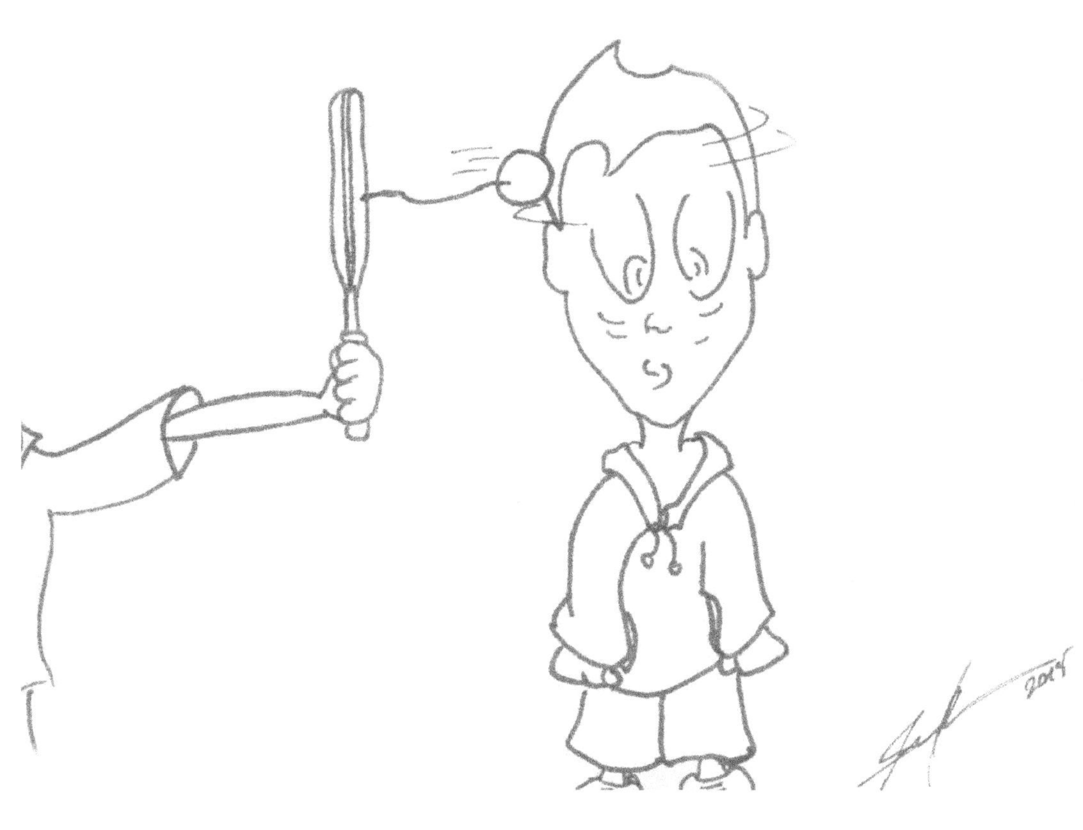

"Duh"

1) My understanding is that healthy eating is an easy and practical way to ensure a long and happy life, but at what point do we need to draw the line?

At first we were condemned for being carnivores. Then we were ostracized for being a predaceous member of the food chain. Now it seems that the politically correct way to enjoy a meal is to pay a farmer to let us graze in his field.

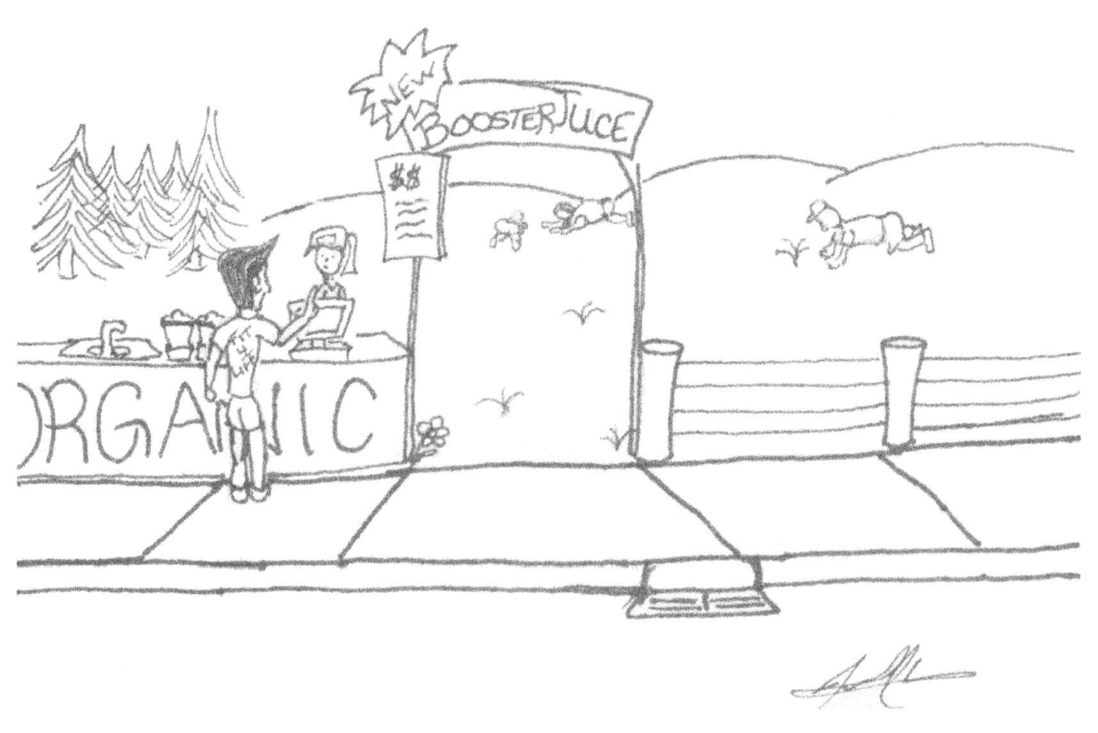

“100% Organic”

2) In elementary school my best friend was promoted to the "smart class" because he was able to recite multiples of twelve on a whim. I, on the other hand, was catalogued as a satisfactory child because I was having difficulty differentiating between the different types of trees in the forest.

This vague line between the intellectually elite and the common dunce was blurred when the screeching sounds of the doors to the information highway grated our ears. Back then, all my questions could be answered by asking Jeeves.

I wonder, what ever happened to my beloved internet butler?

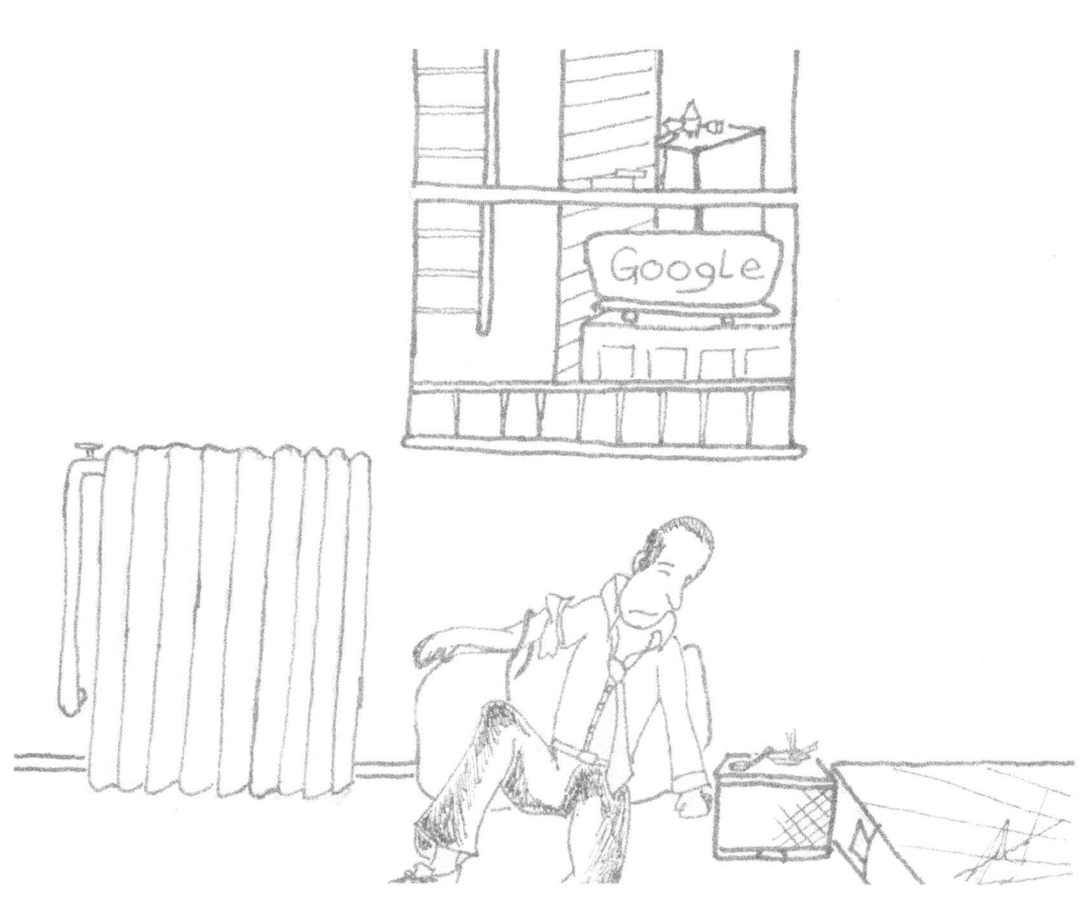

“Jeeves”

3) One day I want to look back and utter the words “I was there!” I want to be able to tell the story of my experience and boast about how amazing it was to be one of the only people to witness an event. And I want to lie about the details to make myself seem cooler than I actually am.

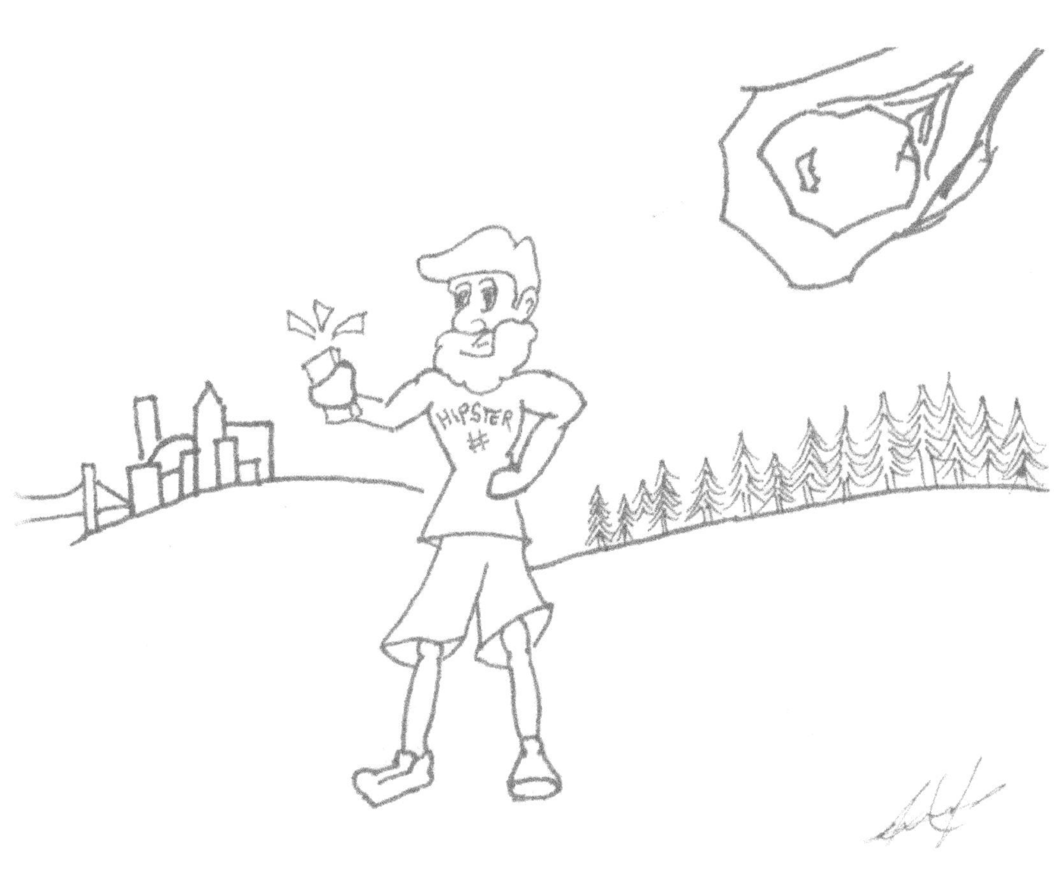

"Hipster's Last Selfie"

4) It seems we've been stretching the meaning of certain words these days. Or maybe it does take a genius to figure out how to clear my browser history?

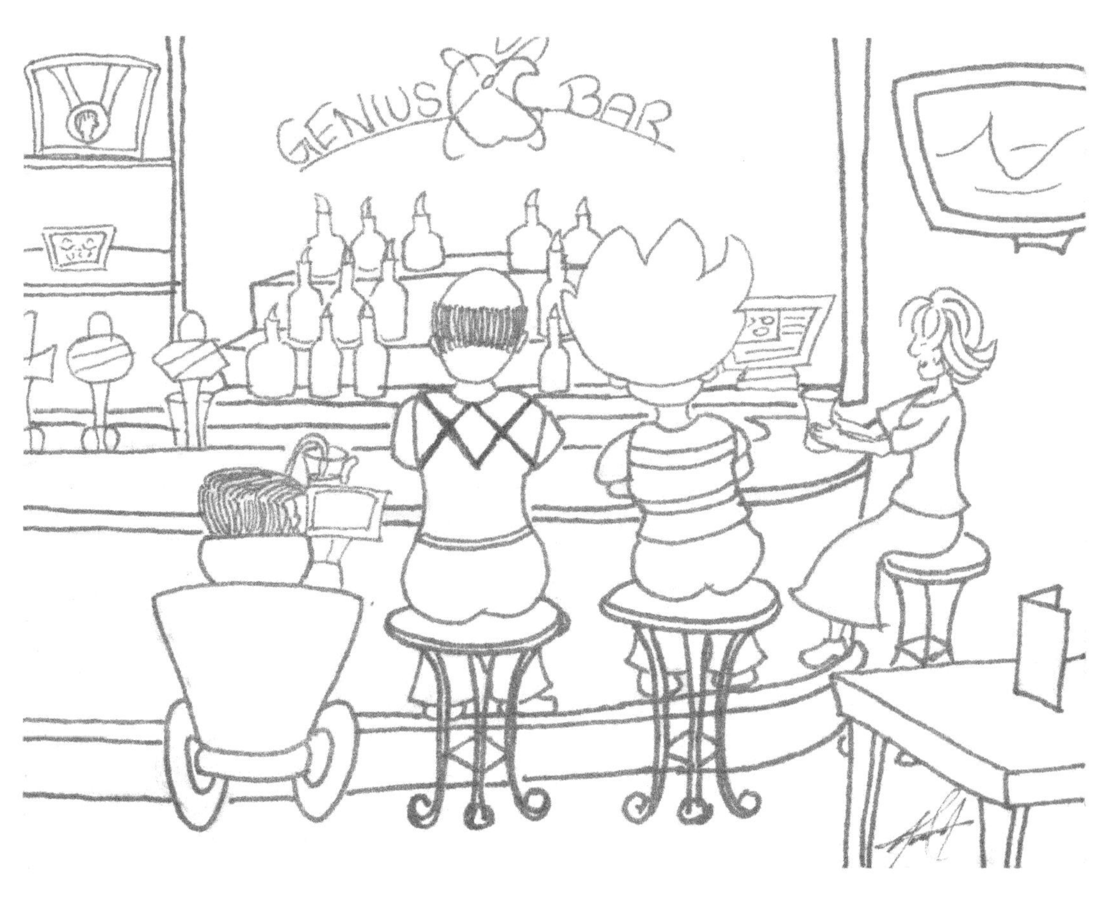

"Genius Bar"

5) I also would like to point out that given today's standards in linguistics, I think I should have gotten an A in high school English. #somuchforEQAO

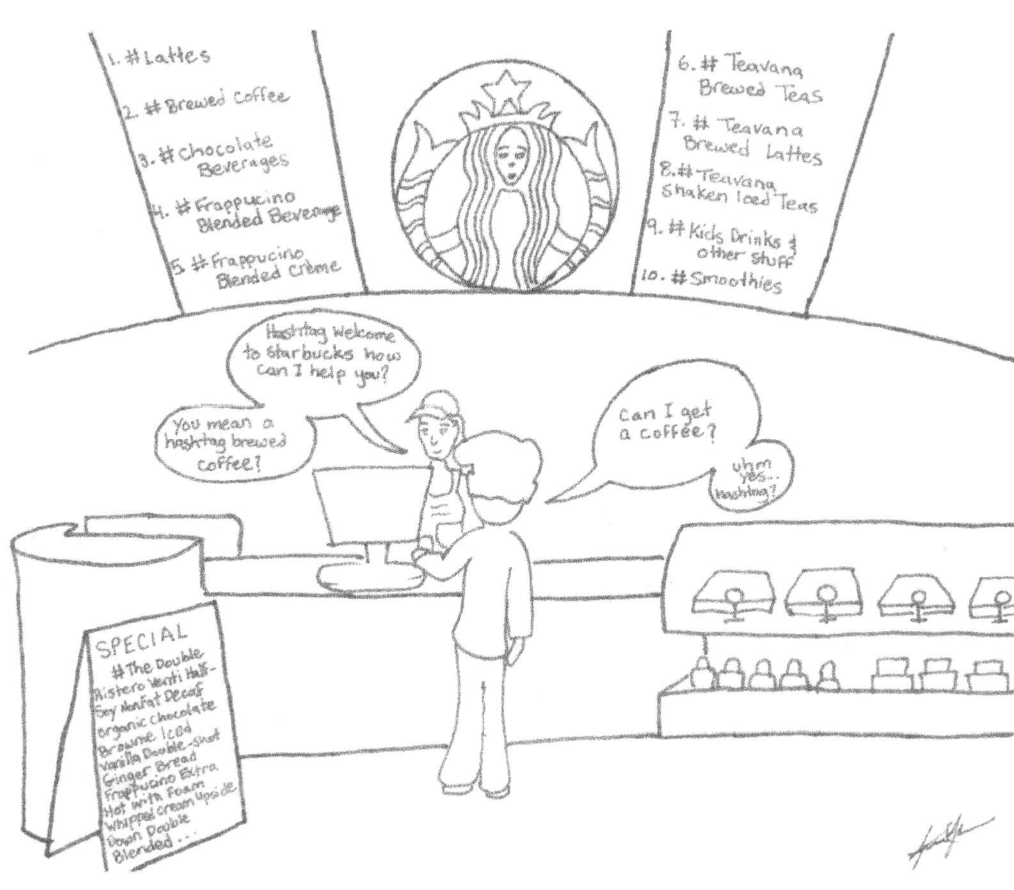
1. #Lattes
2. #Brewed Coffee
3. #Chocolate Beverages
4. #Frappucino Blended Beverage
5. #Frappucino Blended Crème
6. # Teavana Brewed Teas
7. # Teavana Brewed Lattes
8. # Teavana Shaken Iced Teas
9. # Kids Drinks & other stuff
10. # Smoothies
Hashtag Welcome to Starbucks how can I help you?
Can I get a coffee?
You mean a hashtag brewed coffee?
uhm yes... hashtag?
SPECIAL
#The Double Ristero Venti Half-Soy Nonfat Decaf organic chocolate Brownie Iced Vanilla Double-shot Ginger Bread Frappucino Extra Hot with Foam Whipped cream Upside Down Double Blended . . .

"#Orderup"

Despite all these things, I still think this world can be pretty cool sometimes. And who knows, perhaps we're all still O.K. in God's eyes.

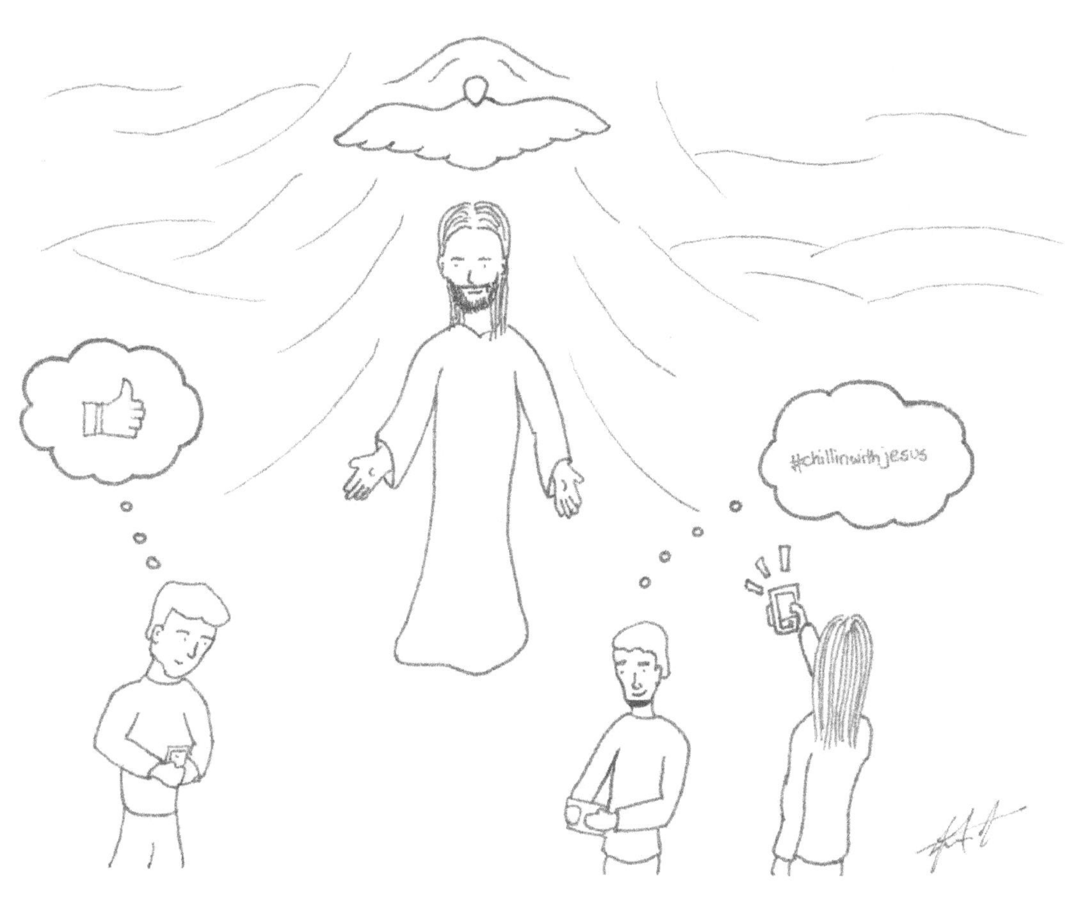

"The Second Coming"

That is, until it all comes to an end.

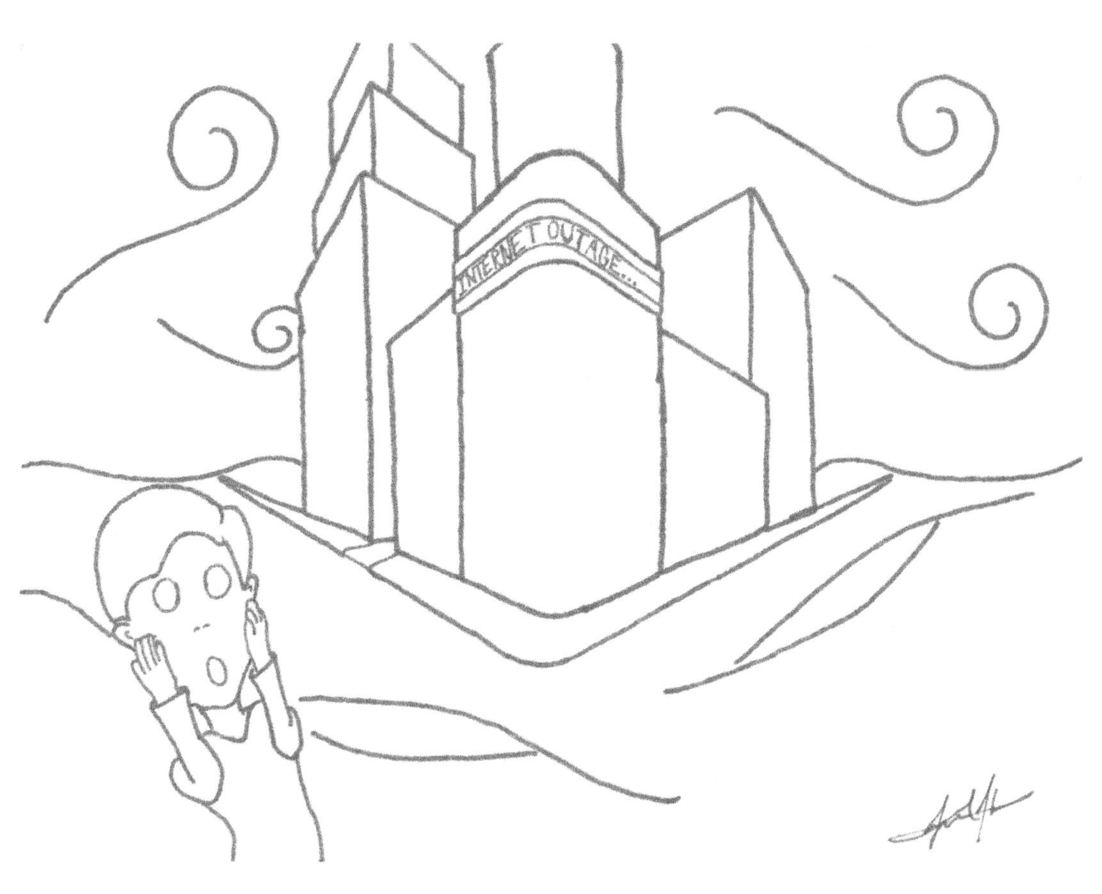

"Internet Outage - The Horror"

PART 3

He Loves Me, He Loves Me Not

There's nothing like the first date with the person you're going to spend the rest of your life with.

First you meet in a public place to avoid being murdered by this stranger who you know nothing about. Then you make awkward conversation with many prolonged moments of silence. Followed by the obvious half-assed attempt to woo them before they completely lose interest. And finally, the night is topped off with a botched first kiss that will never be forgotten for the rest of your lives.

And even if all of these things go well, you're still subject to mandatory time in the Friend-Zone.

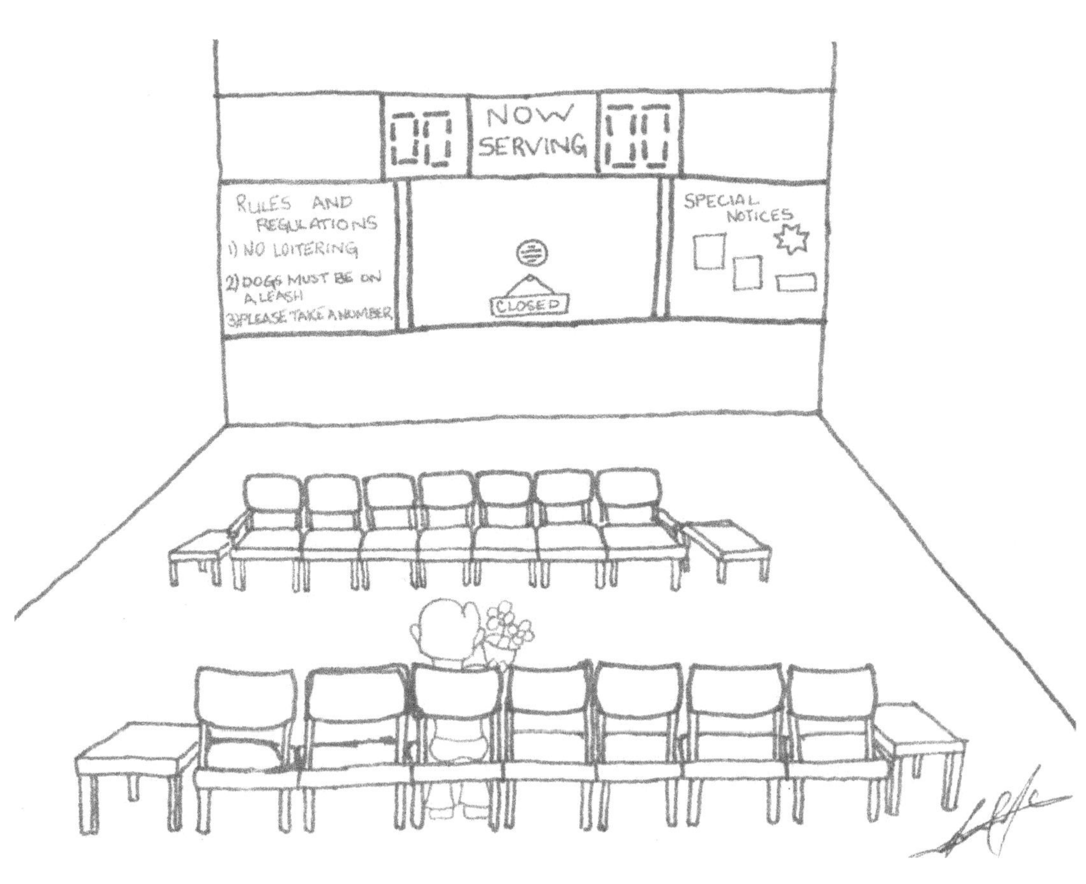

"Waiting For Her"

But then it happens. You get a late night text from them and it makes your heart skip a beat. At first you're nervous, then you're calm, then you're mad, then you're upset, then you realize you've gone through every emotion before finally reading the message.

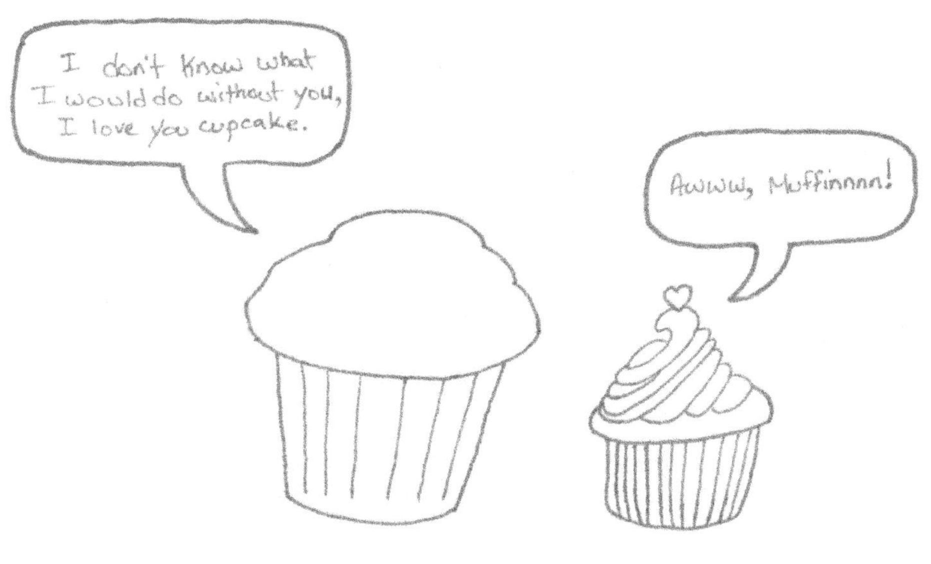

"Culinary Soap Opera"

Although you're jumping for joy on the inside, you pretend to be suave and sophisticated, responding vaguely to try hiding the fact that in your mind you're already planning your wedding.

And being the cool cat that you are, you flirt to try and ease them into showing you who they really are under all those layers of insecurity.

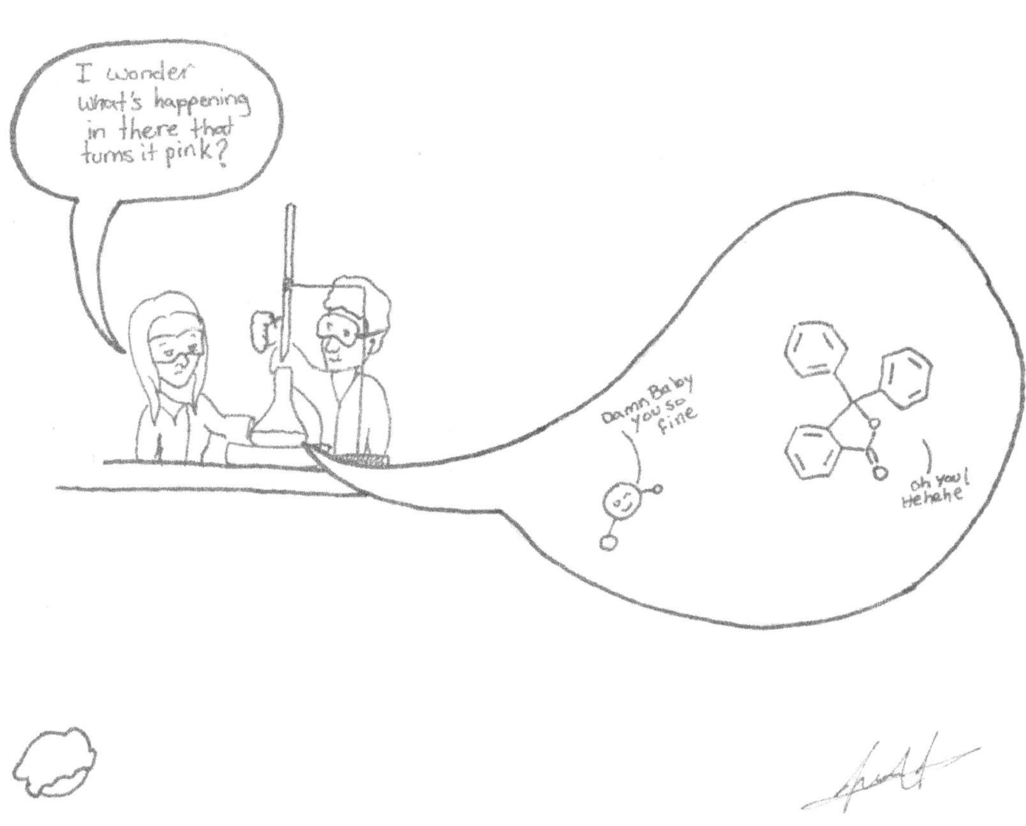

"Feel The Chemistry"

Soon you learn about all their dirty little secrets and guilty pleasures, and that you shouldn't get between them and the last slice of pizza when they're hungry.

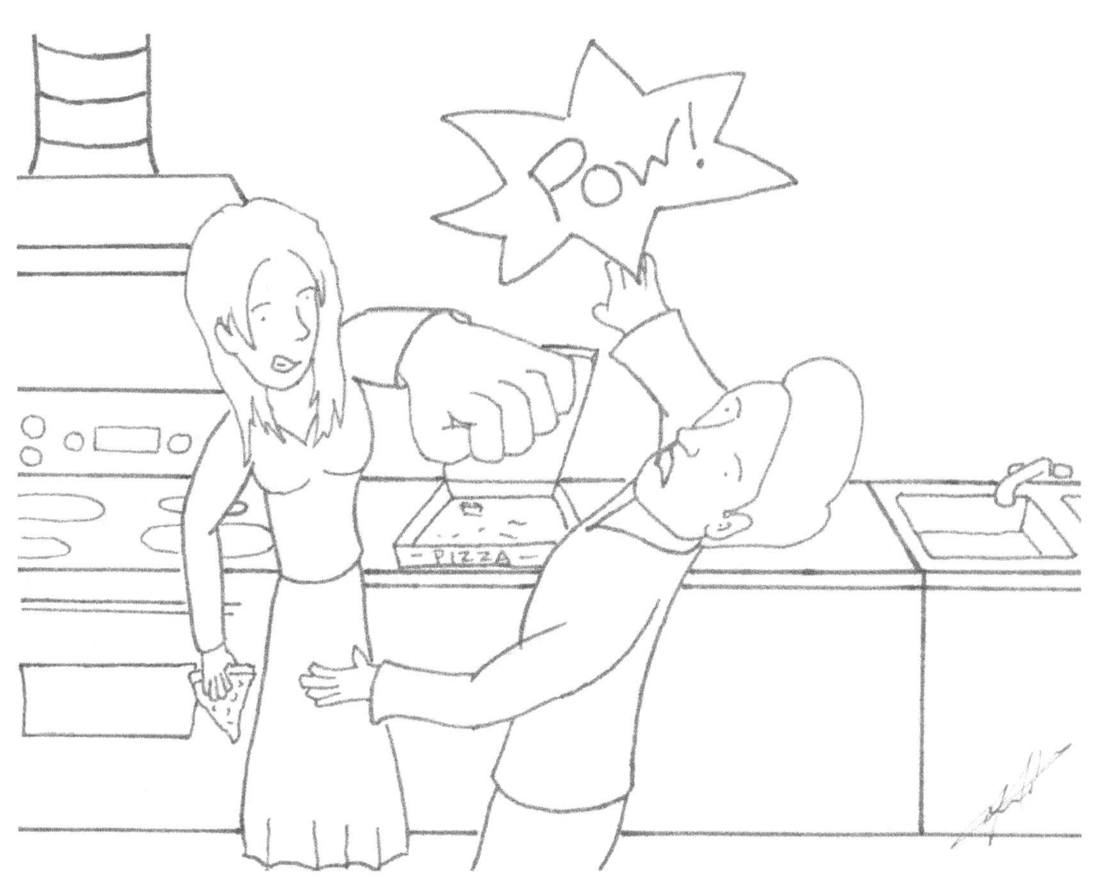

"Love Till The Last Slice"

And after all that is said and done, and all the time you've spent together, and all the promises you've made to each other, you realize that maybe they're just not the one.

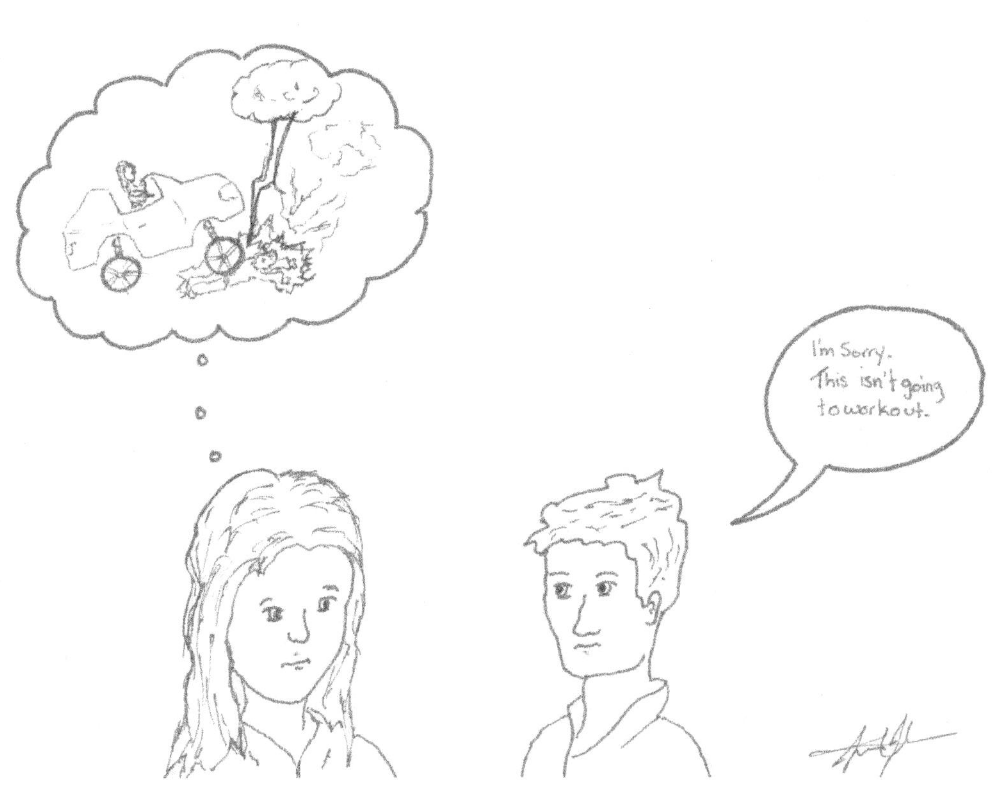

"The Break-Up"

So you climb back into your bubble, after rebuilding your wall of insecurities and begin to mend your broken heart. Until the next person you meet steps up to bat, and you're in love all over again.

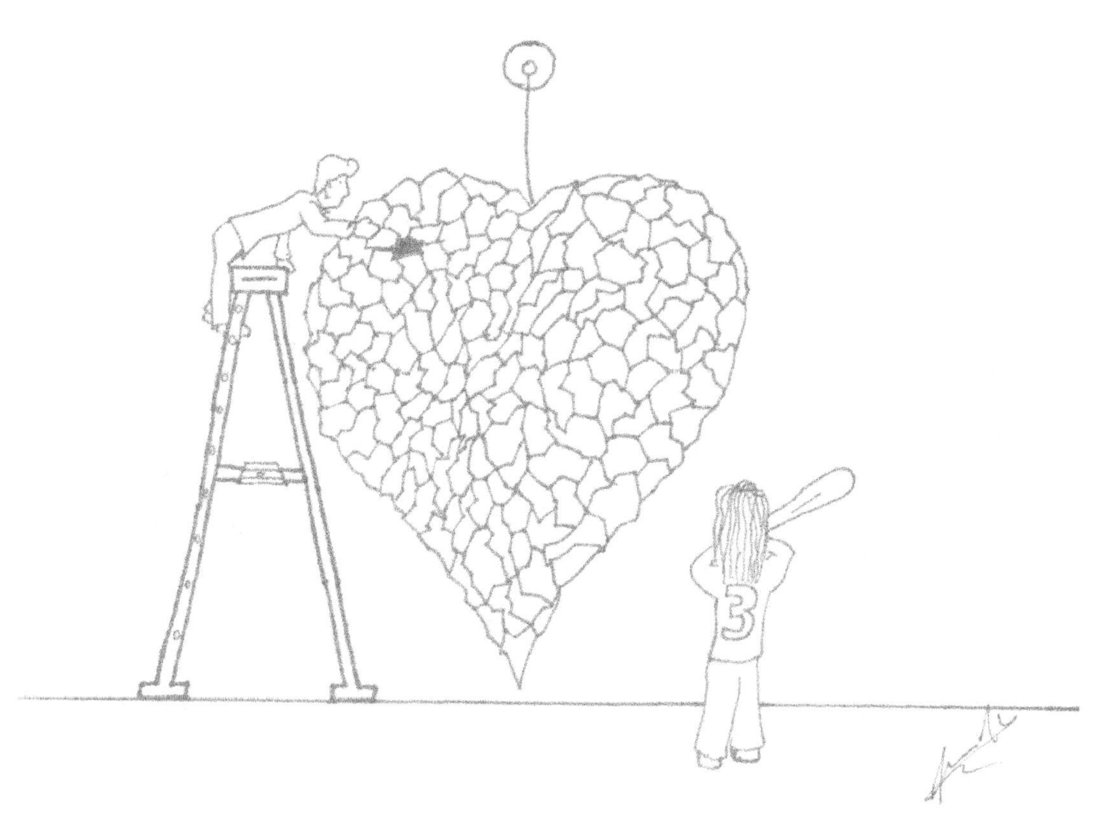

"Next To Bat"

PART 4

I Before E, Except After C

Oblivion is bliss. It's an overused and underrated saying. I didn't really understand the meaning of this quote until I learned to think beyond the extent of my education. Everyday for sixteen years I was told that I must complete my homework and keep up with my readings. I needed to memorize dates and formulas, and I was repeatedly evaluated on my ability to regurgitate facts. After many sleepless nights, a couple of mental breakdowns and numerous alcohol binges, I finally realized that I simply wasn't meant to be a straight-A student. I love learning, I pursue knowledge on a daily basis, not because I have to, but rather, because I want to.

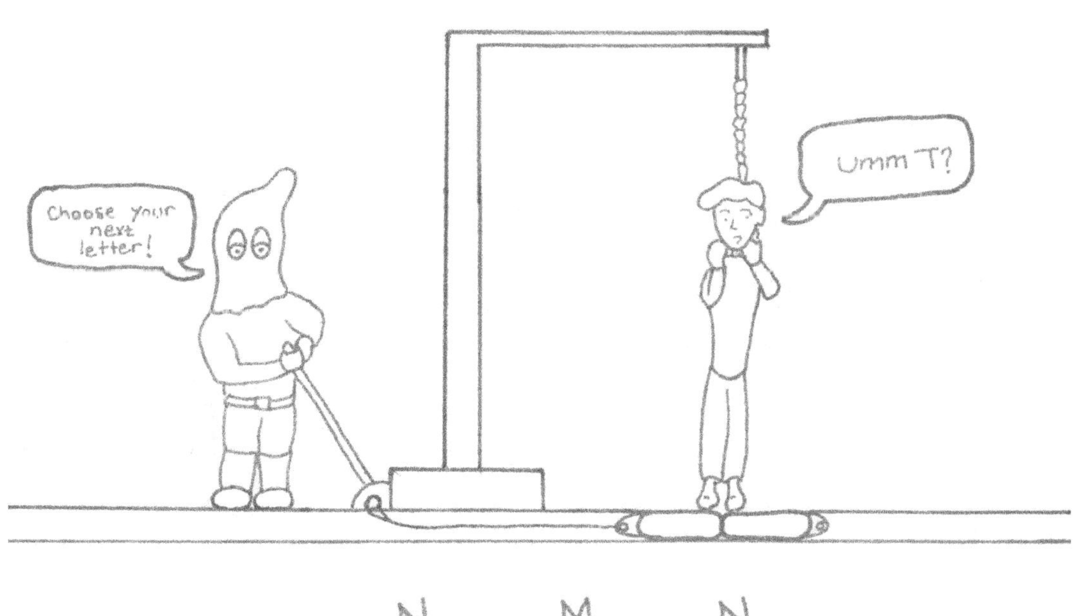

"Let's Play A Game"

I'm not the only one who hates school. I spent the majority of my student career daydreaming about my teachers doing a funny dance in front of the class, or being chased down the halls of my school by a group of super secret assassins, who were sent by a warlord to eliminate me while I tried to complete a highly covert operation code named "M.A.T.H." Needless to say, I didn't do very well when I was called upon to answer questions in front of my fellow peers.

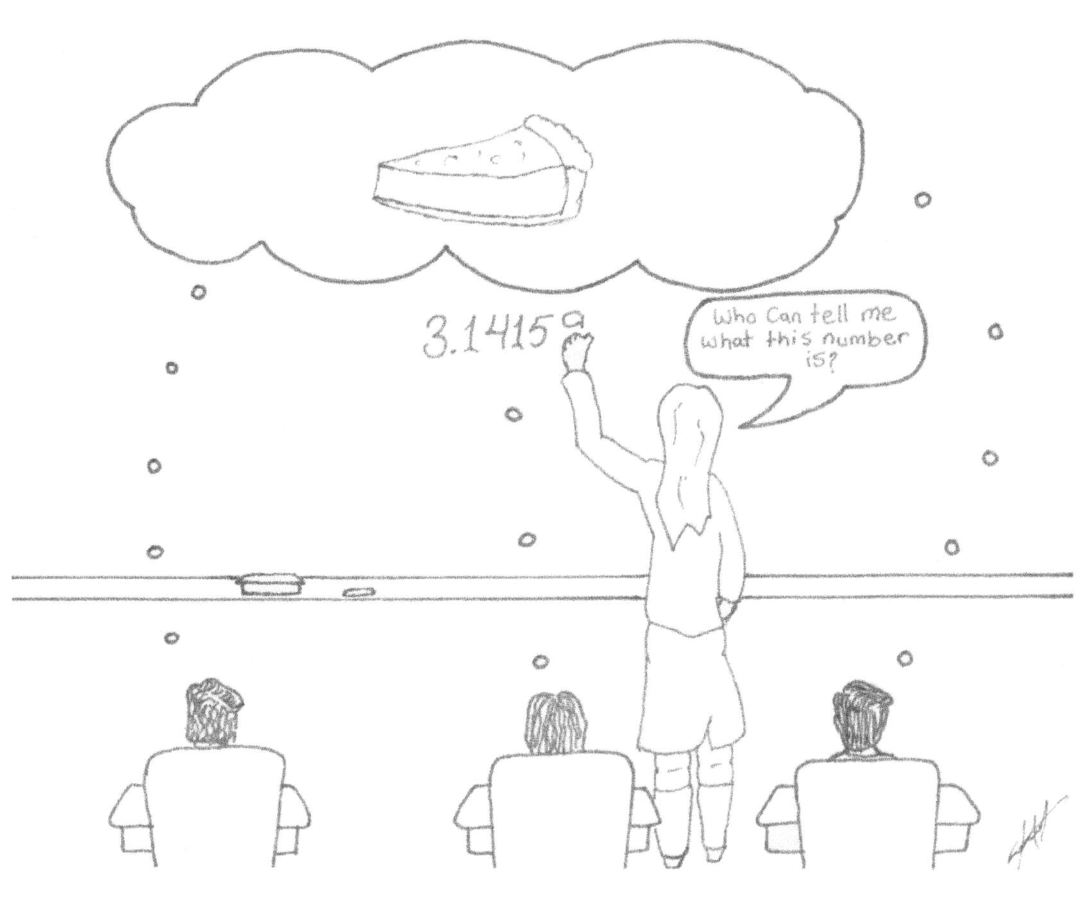

"Mathematical Consensus"

I still somehow managed to make it to university and complete a science degree.

And despite being relieved of all my hopes and dreams in the process, I can safely say I have something to fall back on.

...Or so I'm told.

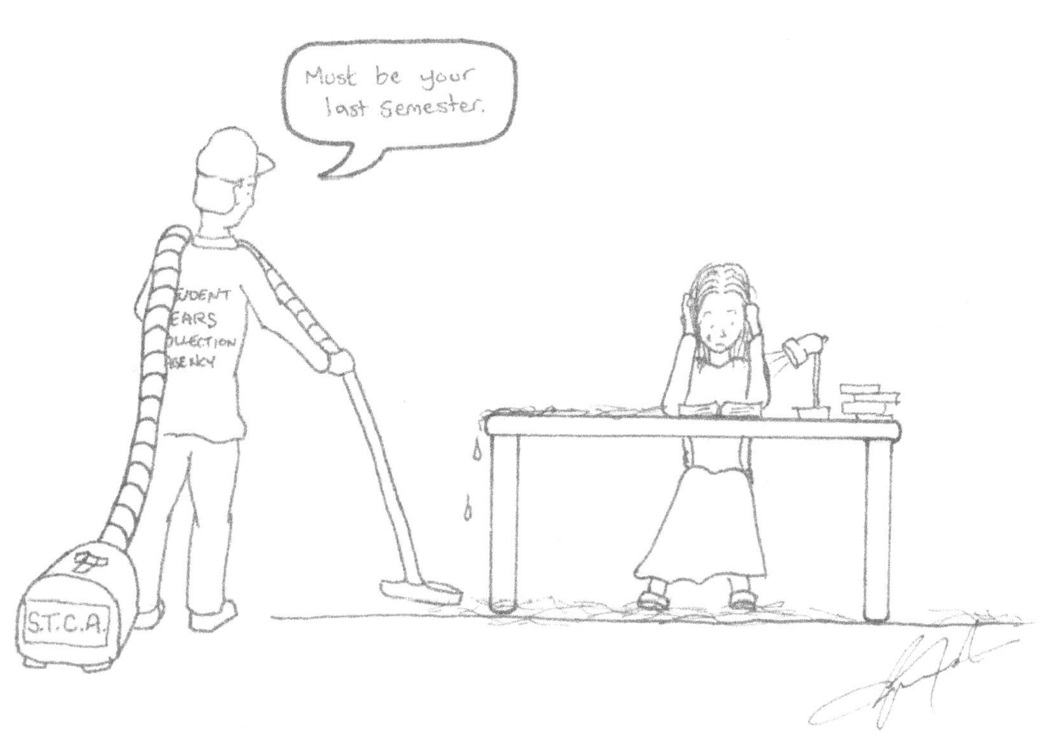

"Student Tears Collection Agency"

Many of my teachers had aspired to become doctors or lawyers or musicians or mechanics, but instead they became teachers. It seems very few people actually want to become a teacher. For most, it's where they end up when they don't have the grades to continue their education, or when they can't find a decent job with their already earned degree or diploma.

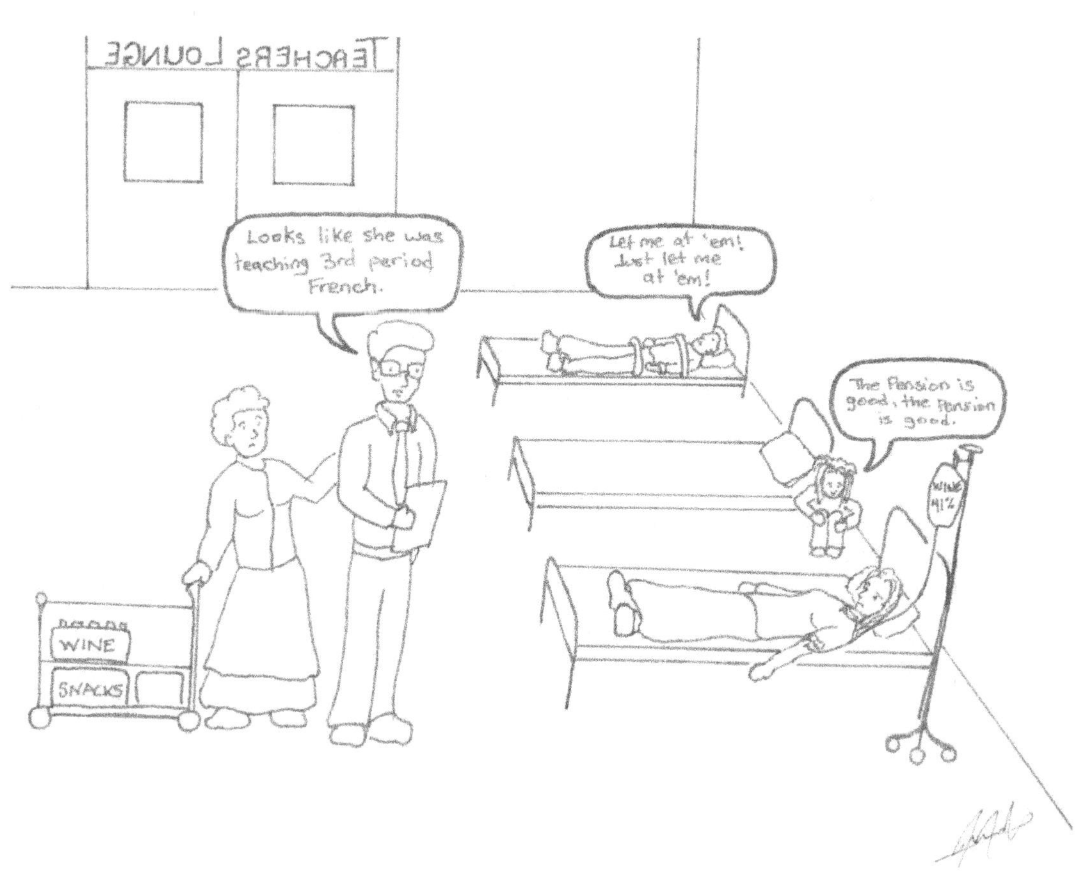

"The 'Teachers Lounge' Ward"

I can't remember the last time there was a full school year without the threat of a teacher strike.

Now, I can understand being in a classroom with a bunch of delinquents isn't the ideal way to spend six hours of the day. Especially if three quarters of them don't want to be there and the other quarter are just there because they hate being at home.

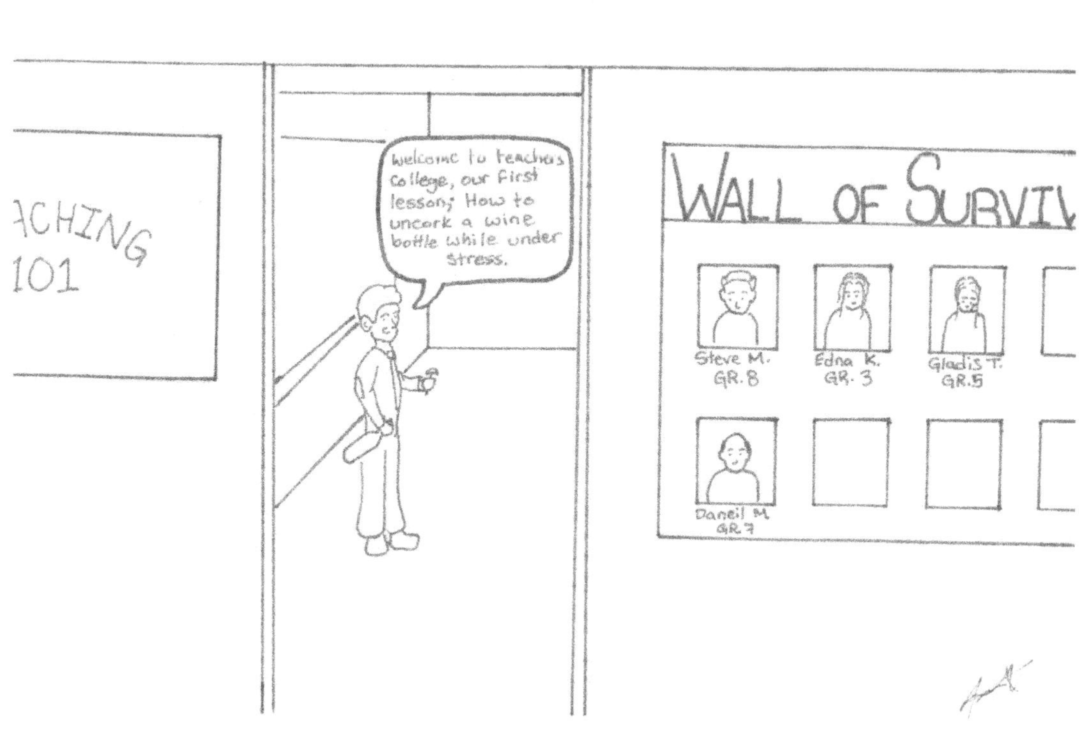

"First Day Of Teacher's College"

But at the end of sixteen years in the education system, I'm rewarded by shaking hands with a person I've never met, in front of people I'll never see again, and walk away with a paper that loses value the moment I step off the convocation stage.

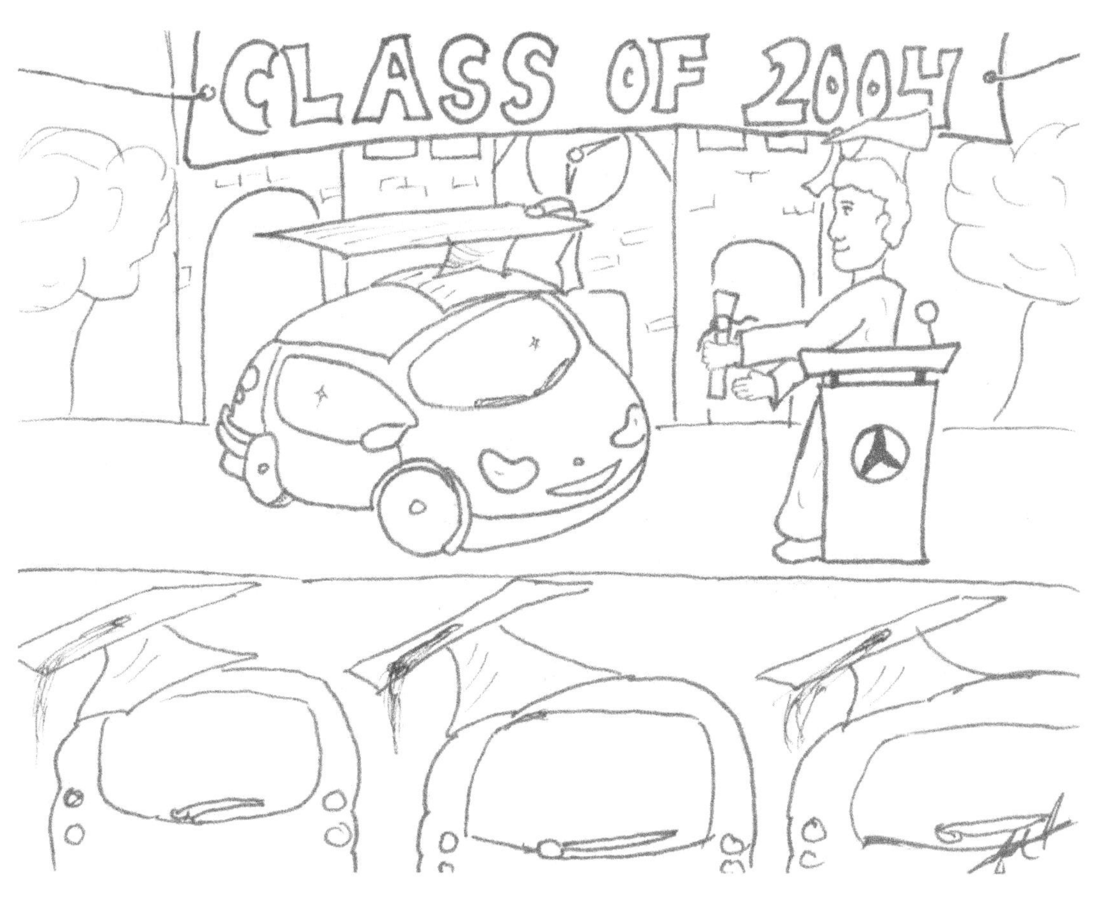

"Smart Car Graduation Day"

And after they've taken away my hope of achieving academic greatness, destroyed my will to pursue my dreams and emptied my pockets to the last dime, I'm tossed into a world that values money over humanity and I'm expected to survive given my costly, "privileged education."

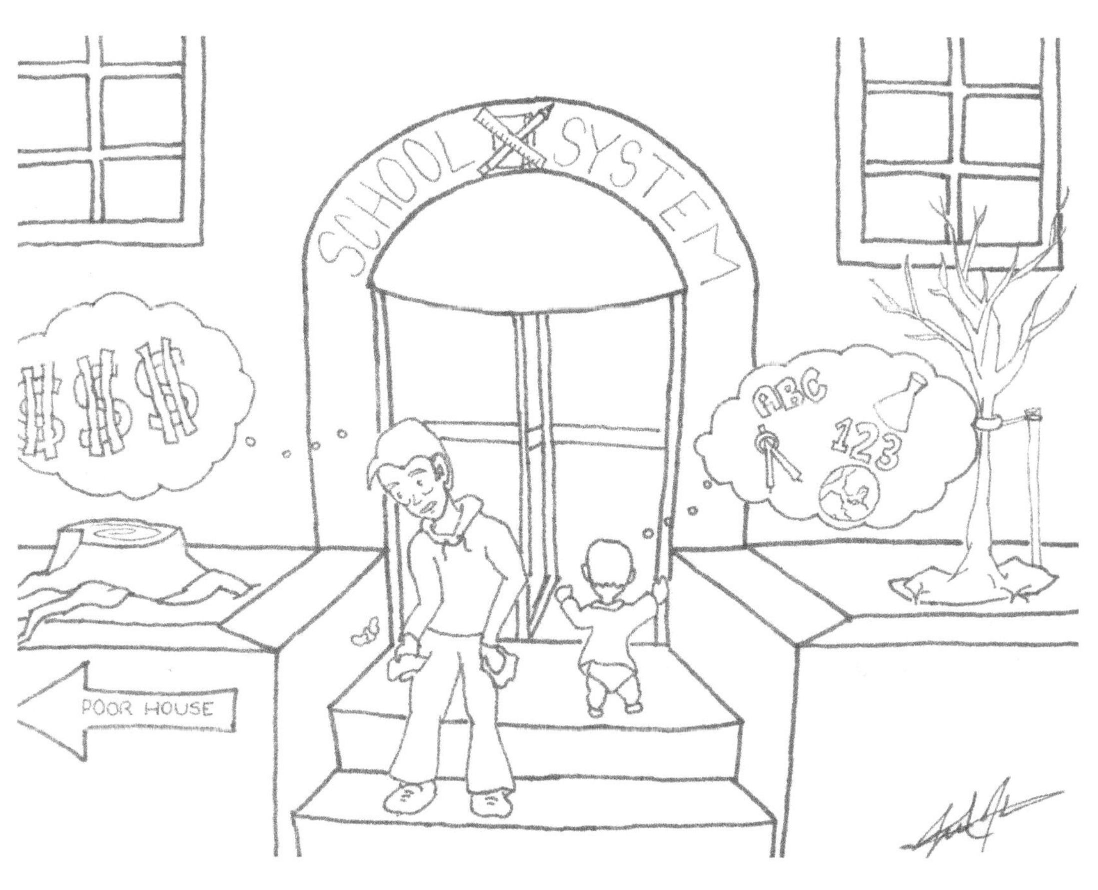

"Higher Education"

PART 5

Entry-Level Oppotunity, Requires 3+ Years Experience

So you've made it through high school, and you've graduated college or university. What next? Get a job? Of course you'd love to walk into the nearest office building, wave your degree and be rewarded for your many years of hard work with a career that will support yourself and your future family. After all, this is why you've been in school for the last sixteen years or more.

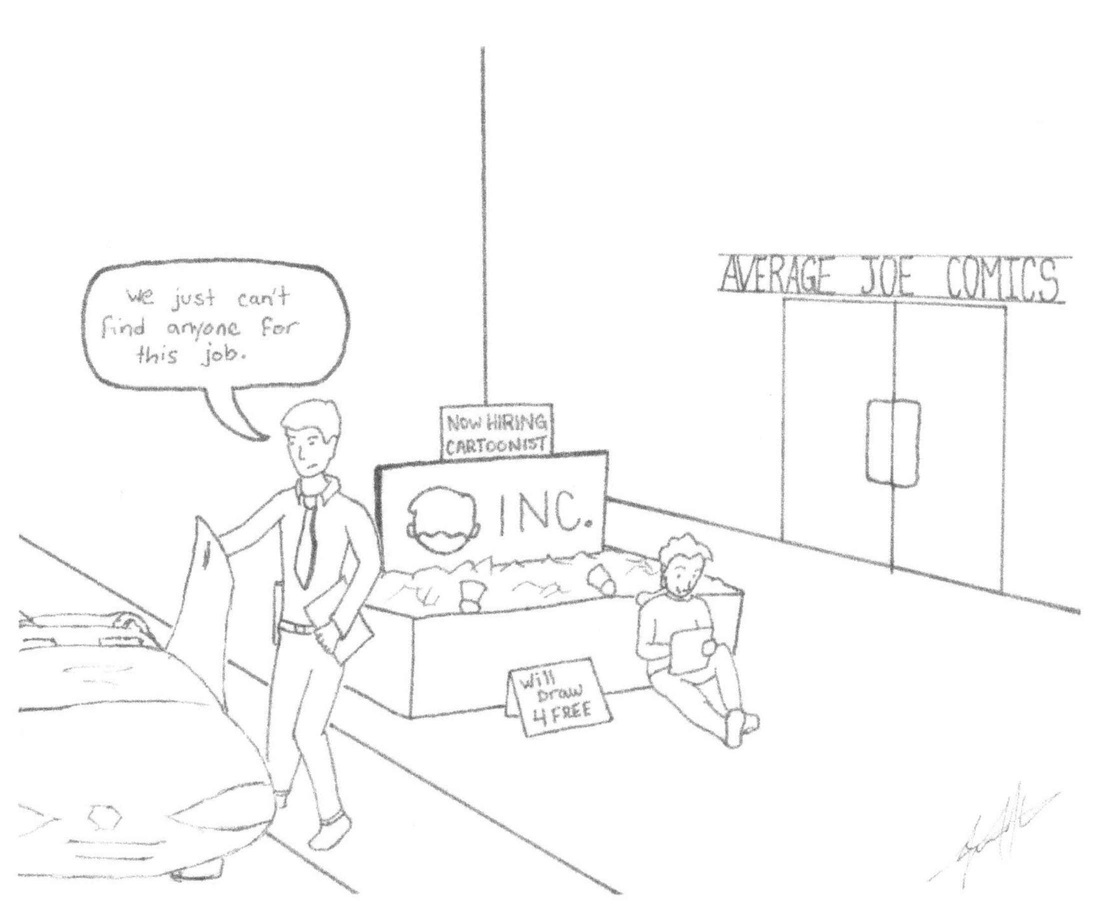

"To Whom It May Concern"

But instead you find yourself sitting at home binge watching TV shows on Netflix, or aimlessly browsing YouTube videos while reading your friends' posts about how they're having a rough day, or how excited they are to go on another vacation, or their adamant stance on a current event. All the while you're trying to convince yourself that you're an entrepreneur who simply hasn't found their million dollar idea.

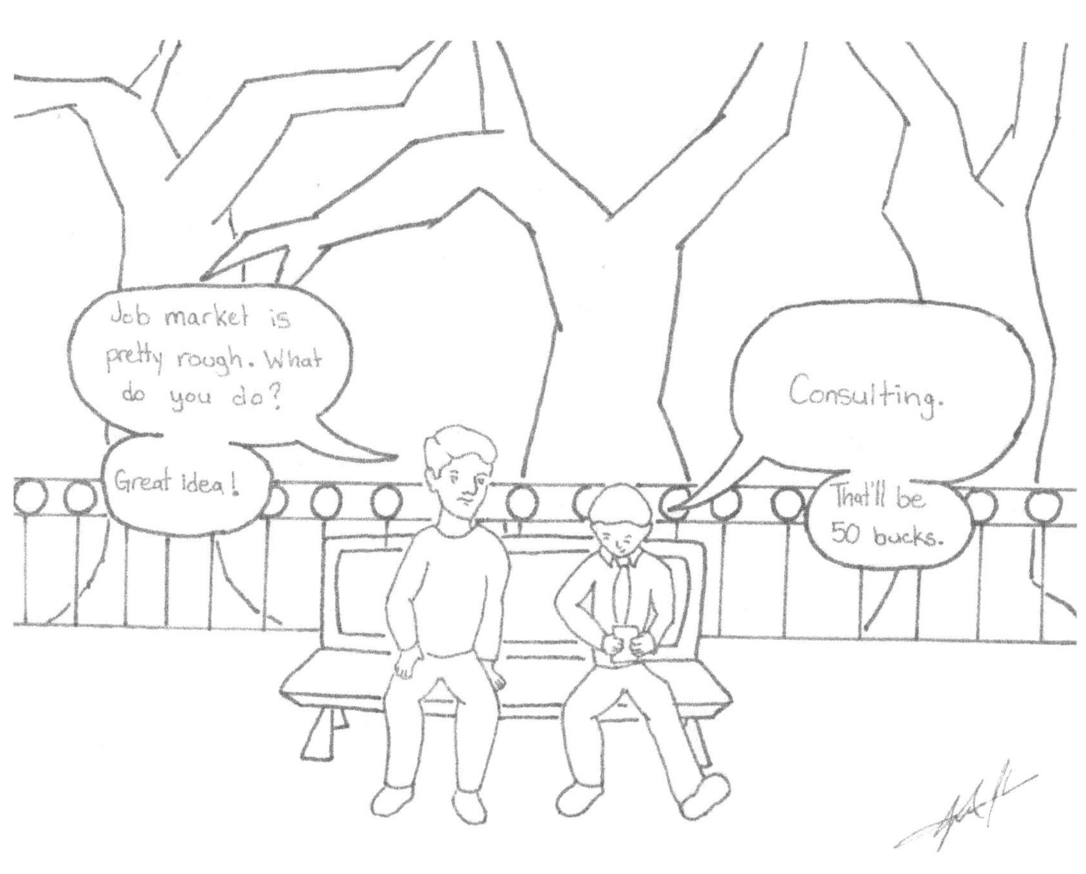

"Free? What's That?"

Eventually, you have to swallow your pride and take up a monotonous job cleaning up after people who assume you're an uneducated or underprivileged individual who fell on hard times and can't seem to get yourself back up on your feet.

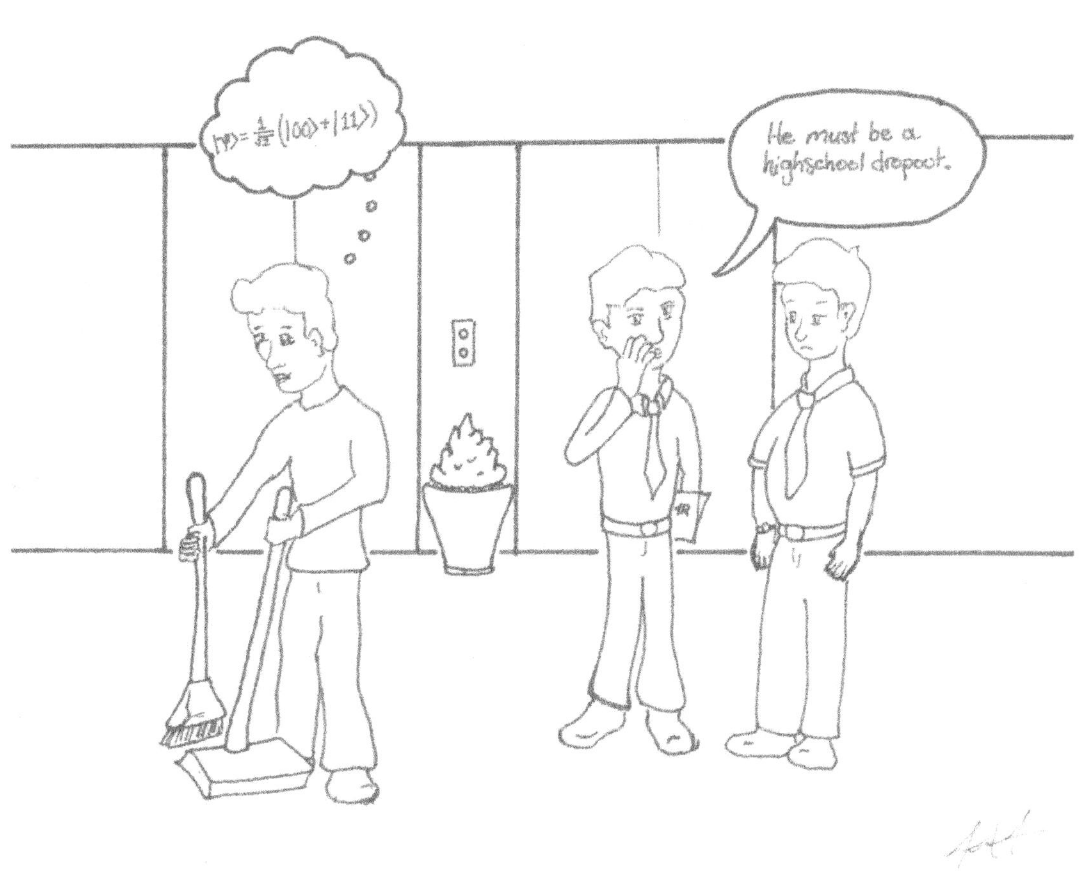
$|\psi\rangle = \frac{1}{\sqrt{2}}(|00\rangle + |11\rangle)$
He must be a highschool dropout.

"Post Doc."

And for the rest of your career you desperately try to climb a figurative ladder that you're swindled to believe will eventually lead to a memorable and fulfilling life.

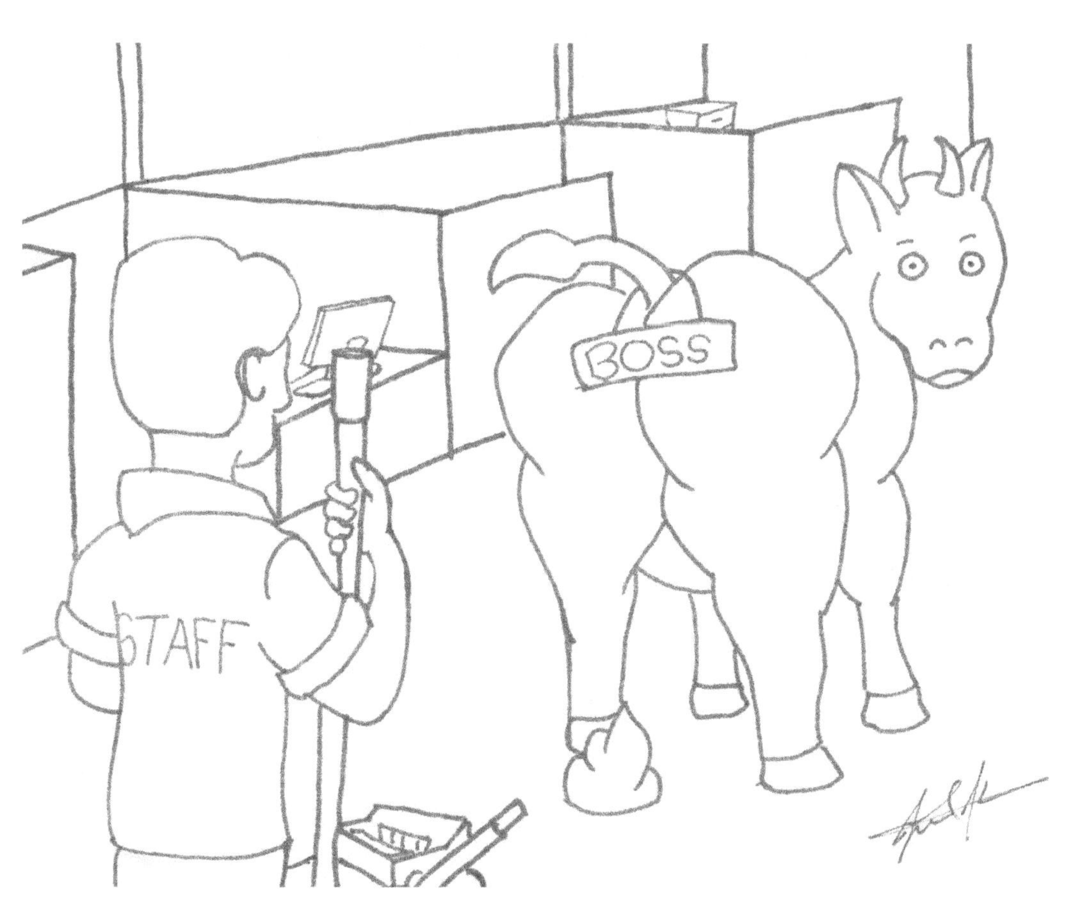

"Dealing With The Boss"

PART 6
Intermission

Have you ever really questioned how the Great Wonders of the World came to be?

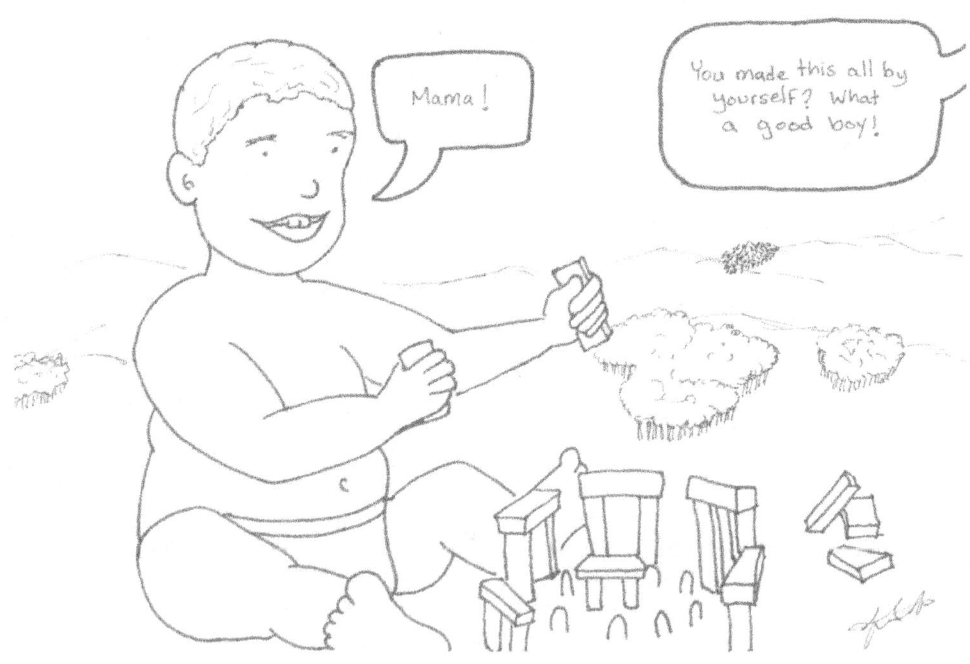

"Stonehenge"

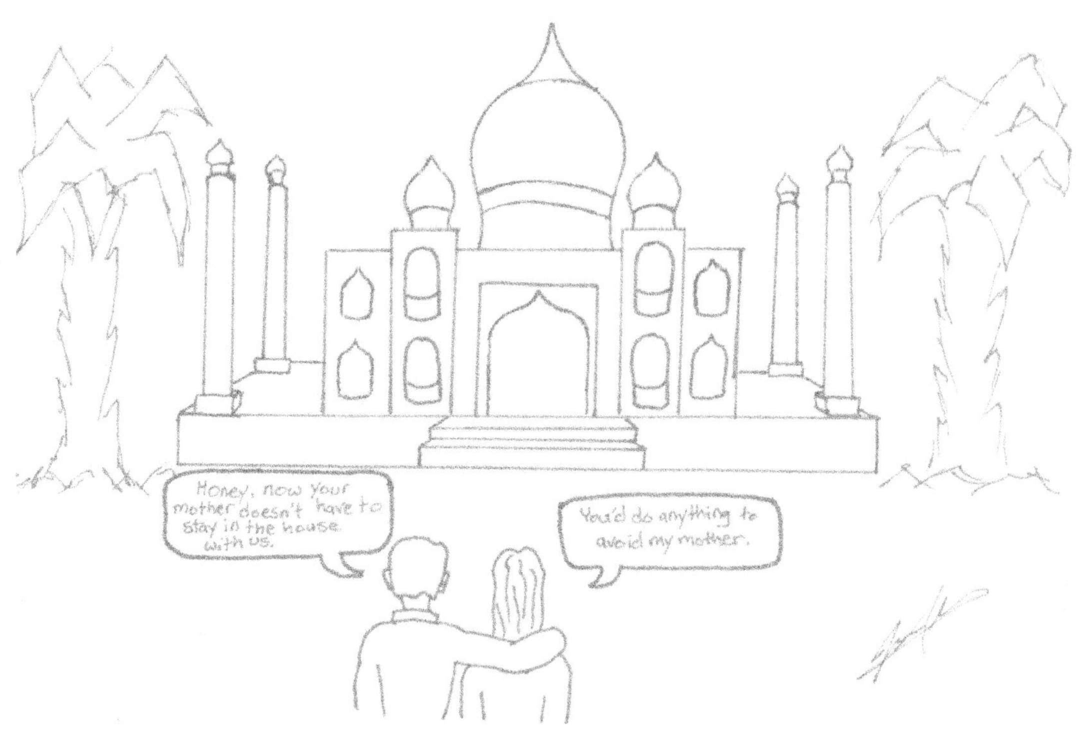

"The Taj Mahal"

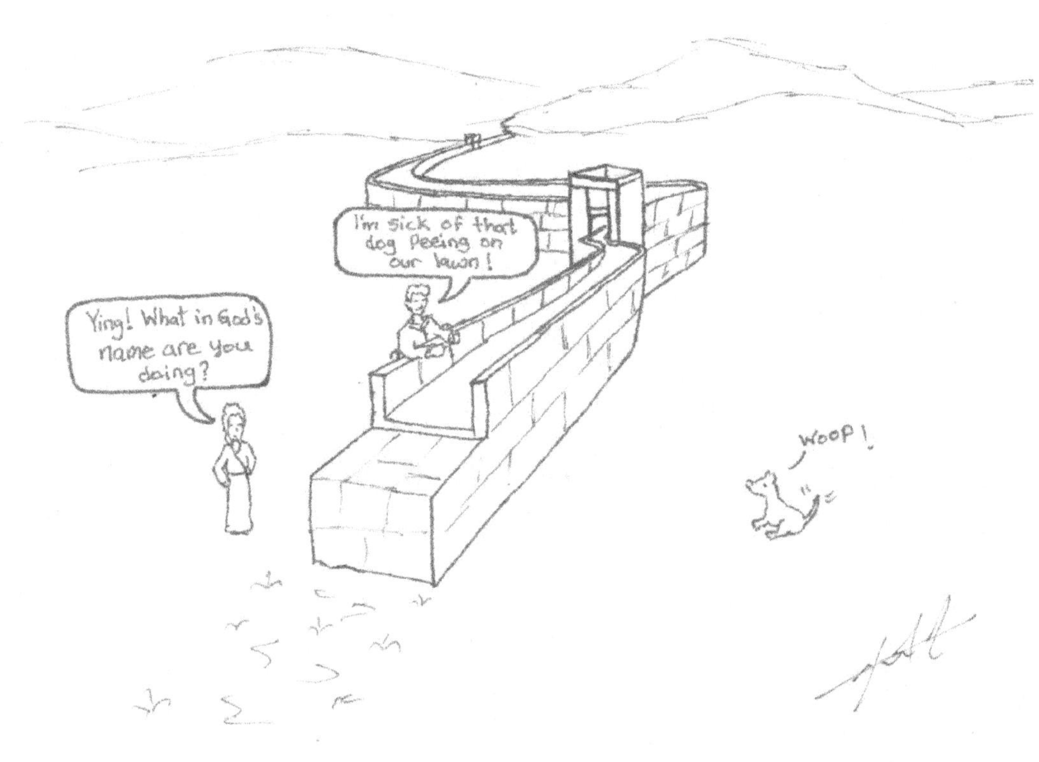

"The Great Wall of China"

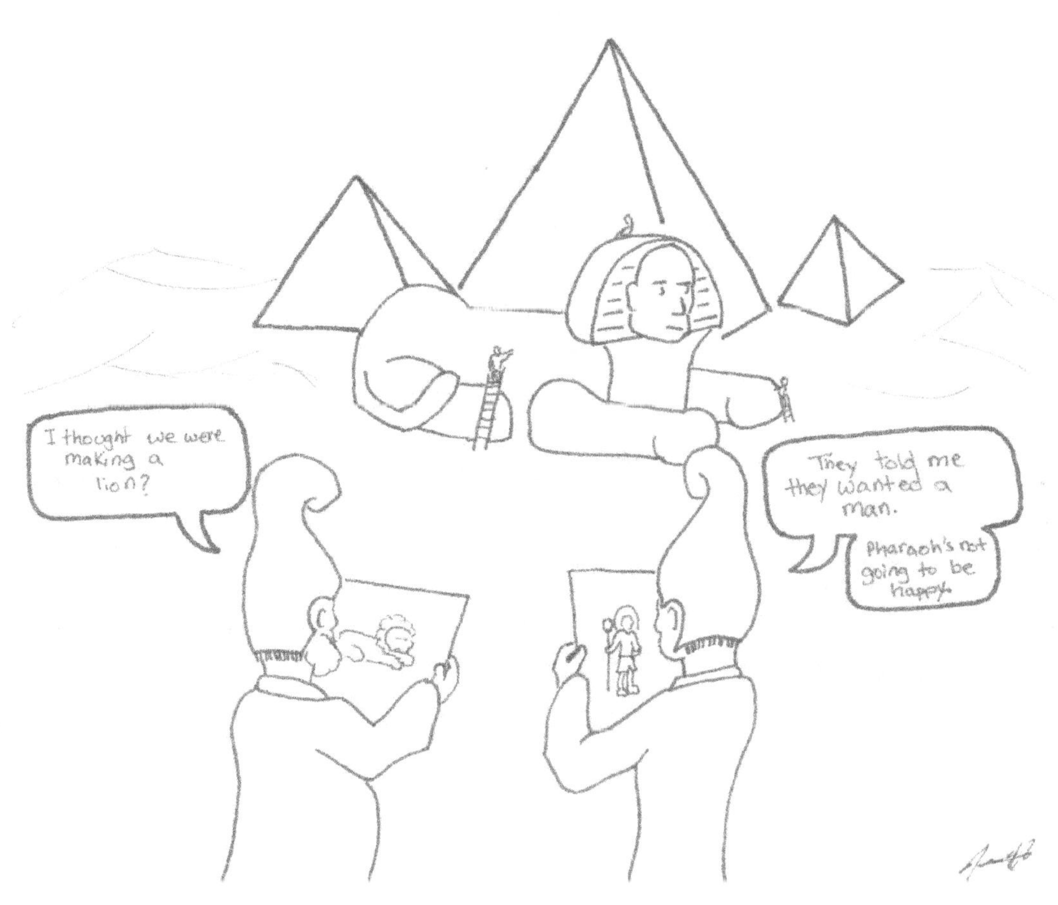

"The Sphinx of Giza"

PART 7

Kids These Days

My parents felt no shame in letting me know that I had made a mistake through foreign parenting techniques. Some might say their ability to implement maximum punishment without receiving retaliation from their offspring was a mastery of the parental arts. But this was during a time when children weren't raised to believe the world owes them something.

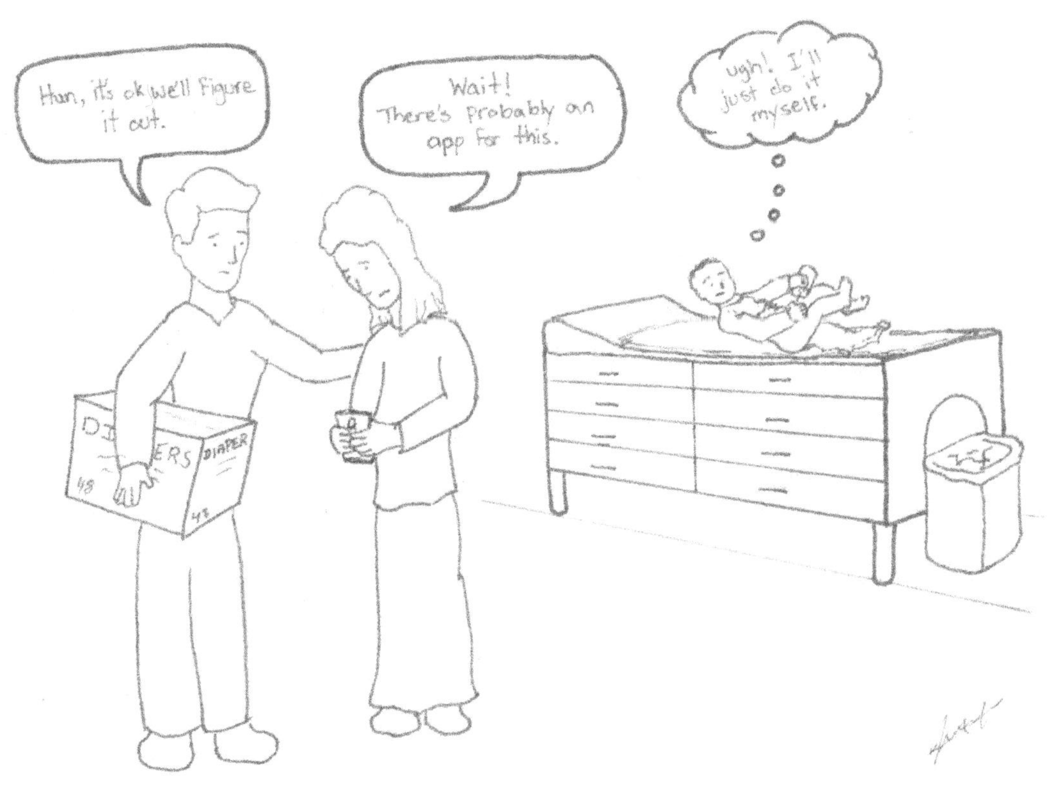

"Parenting Made Easy"

I praise my parents for not being afraid to hit me when I swore or threw a tantrum in public. Because of their discipline I am now able to keep myself in check when I face difficult challenges that test my physical and mental abilities.

Also, the way they portrayed disapproval showed me how to eloquently address my superiors while still expressing my utter distaste for their role in my life.

What I'm trying to say is, parents, don't be afraid to remind your kids who's in charge. They'll thank you for it later.

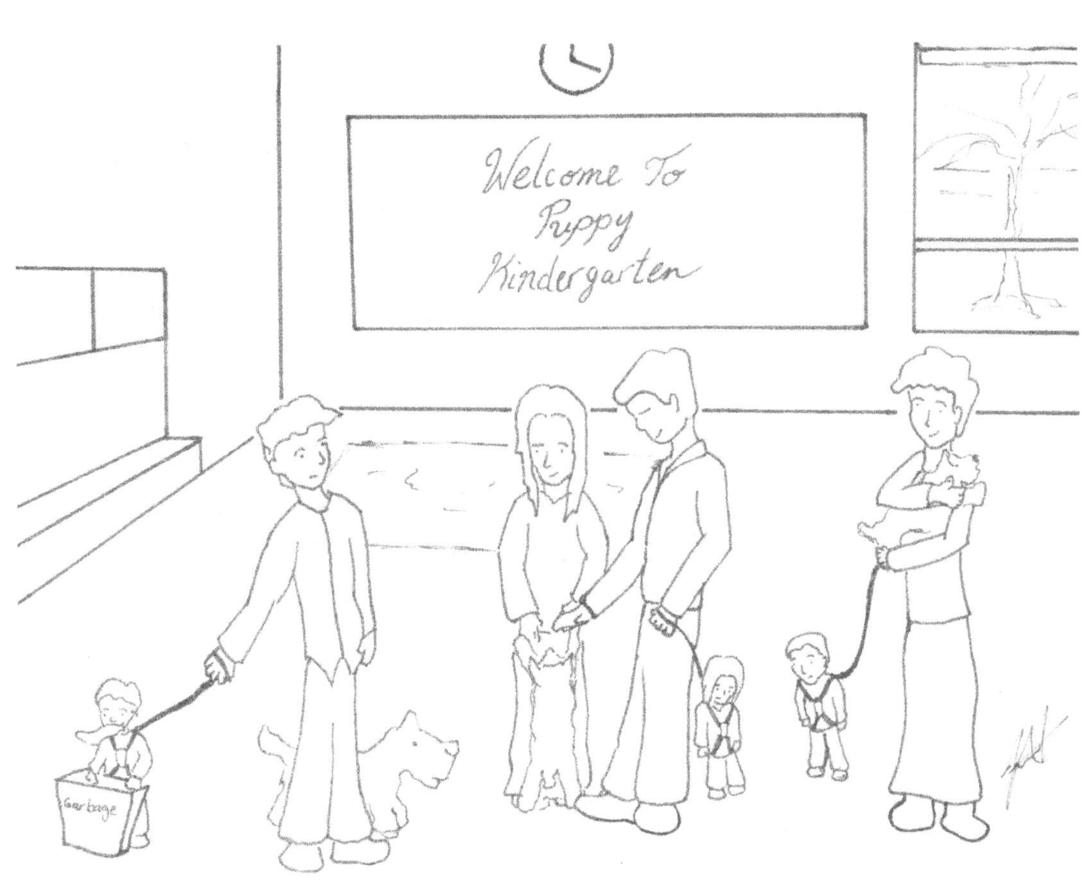

"The First Day Of School"

And hopefully, instead of creating a future society full of anxious, self-important, pompous little brats, we can have strong-minded and well-rounded individuals who aren't afraid to fight for discounted items on Boxing Day.

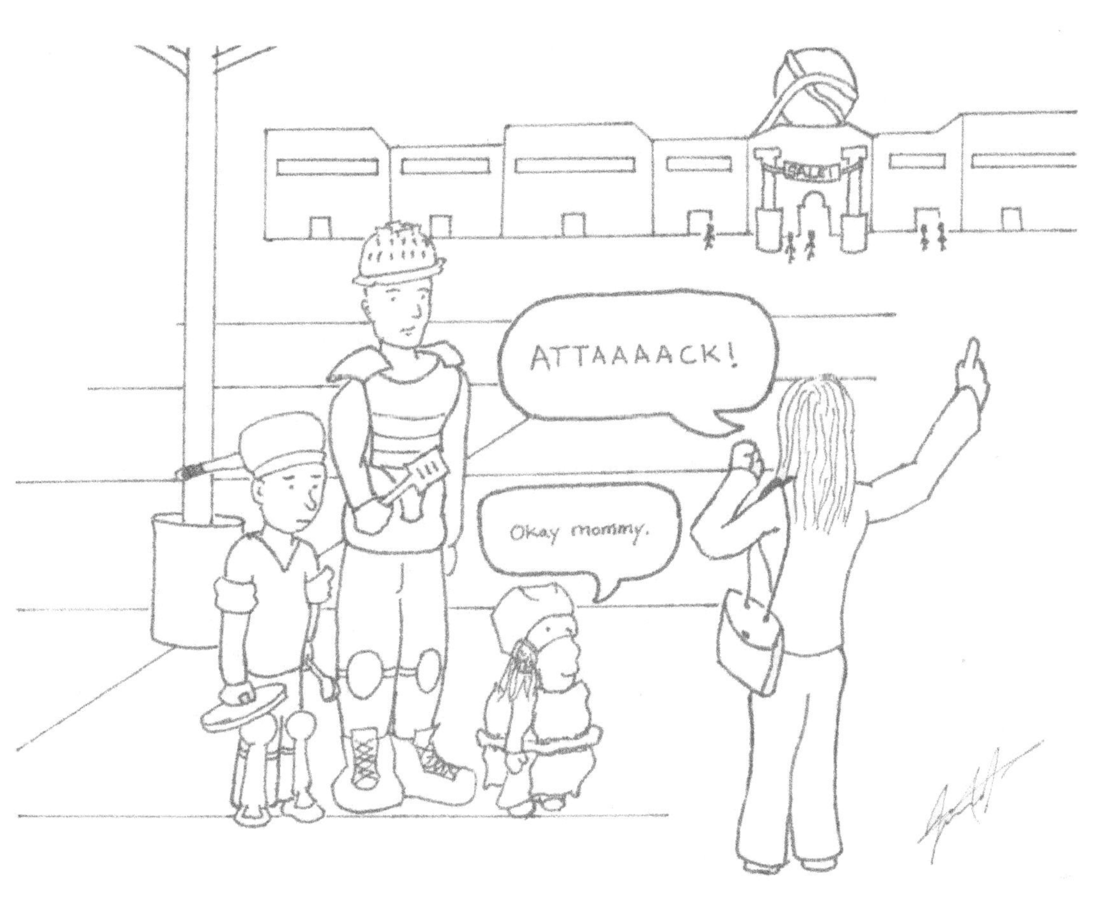

“General Mom On Sale Day”

Part 8

It's The Most Wonderful Time Of The Year

There was a time when I stayed up until 2:00 a.m. on December 25th and looked out of the window in excitement hoping to catch a glimpse of Santa Claus as his sleigh streaked across the sky.

I would lay down on the couch and think about all the questions I wanted to ask him while he took presents out of his big, red bag and arranged them festively around the Christmas tree. Then, I'd imagine giving him a big hug around his big belly before he climbed up through the chimney and flew off into the night.

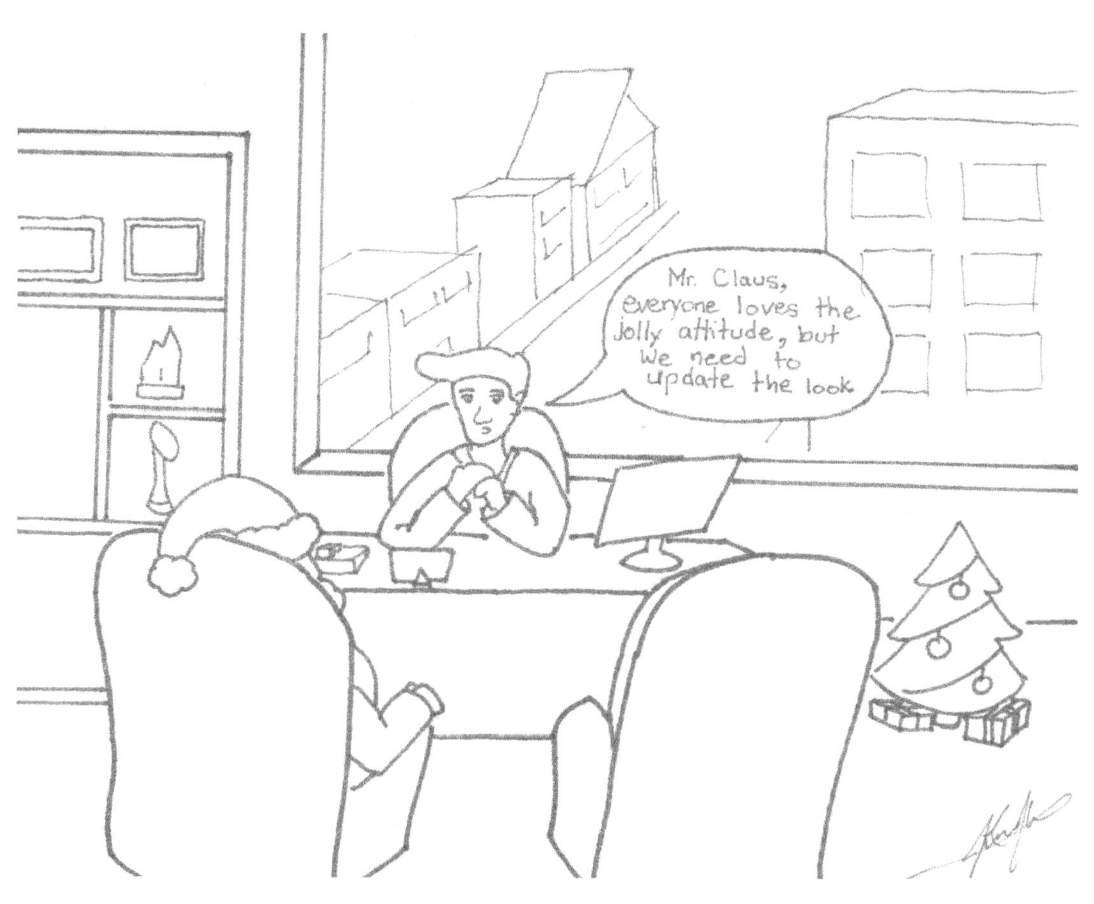

"It's All About The Marketing"

But ever since “The War On Christmas” started, I began to ponder why Santa would want to fly his sleigh over heavily armed countries that possess the capability of shooting down unknown objects flying in restricted airspace.

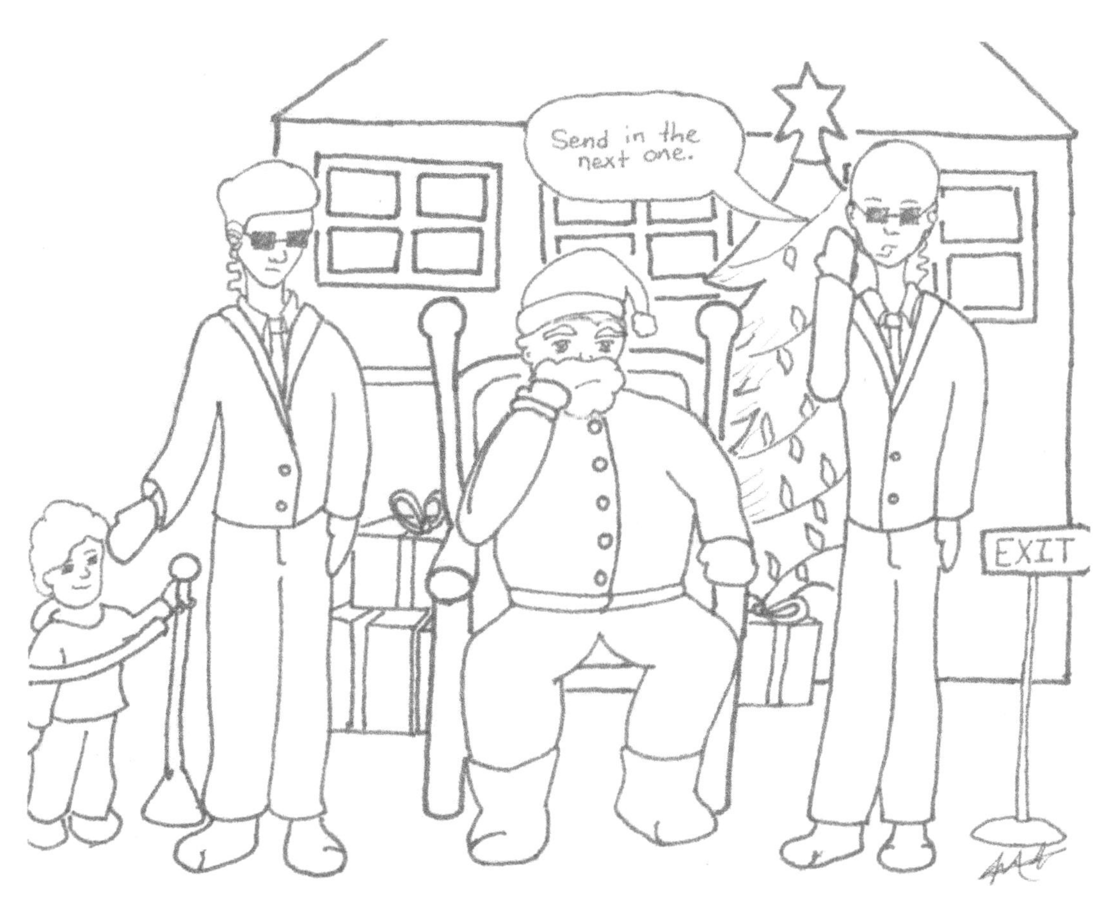

"Coping With The War On Christmas"

So I question, if Santa isn't going to be coming around anymore because of security reasons, who's going to drink all the milk and eat all the cookies left out every Christmas Eve? But more importantly, who's going to bring presents to all the little boys and girls who so desperately tried to be good all year?

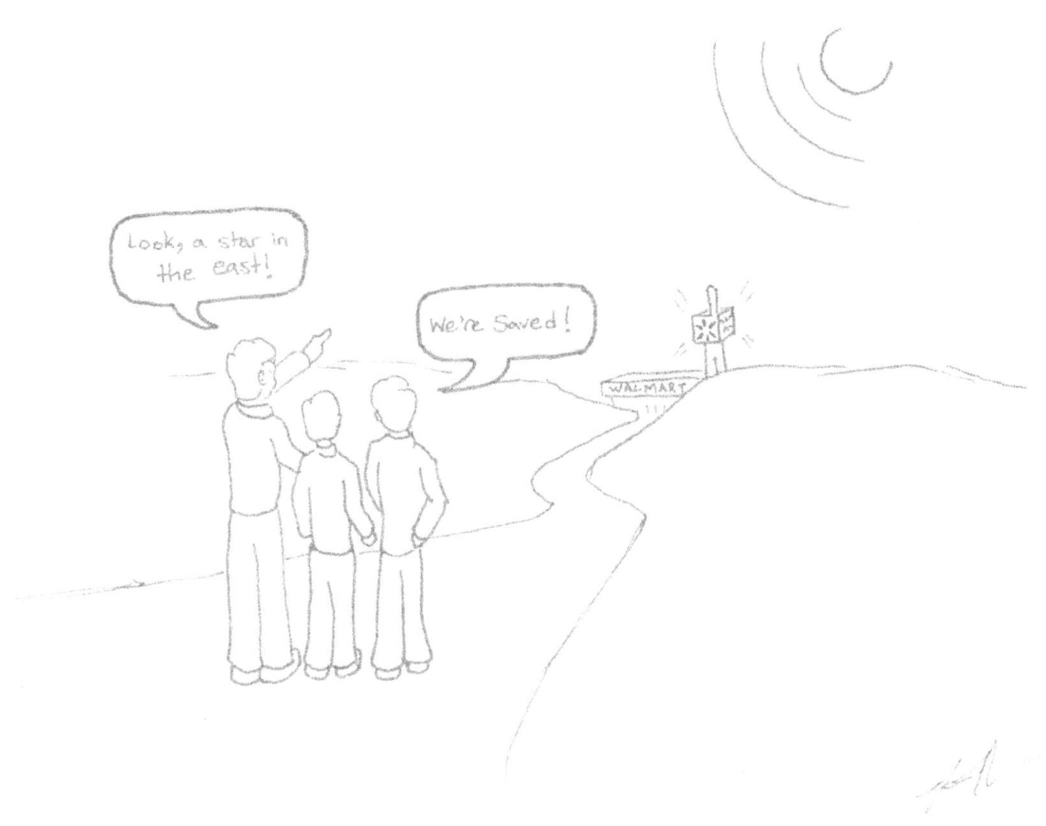

"The Three Unwise Men"

And also, what will all the elves do if there is no longer a need to deliver presents?

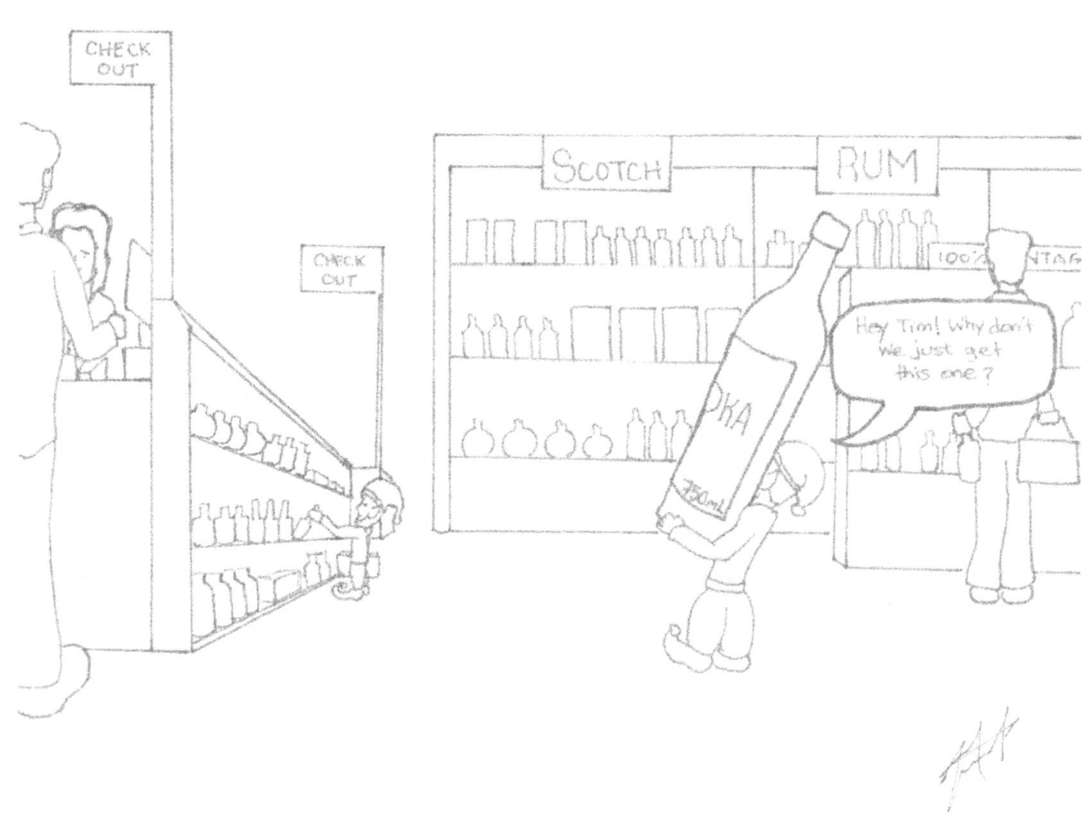

"Mini Bottles"

PART 9
In Conclusion

While most of us would rather stay confined to our bubble and remain oblivious to the self-destructive routine that we've happily accepted as the new norm; I'd like to believe that every once in a while, someone, somewhere, takes a moment to stop everything they're doing and ask, how the hell did we get here?

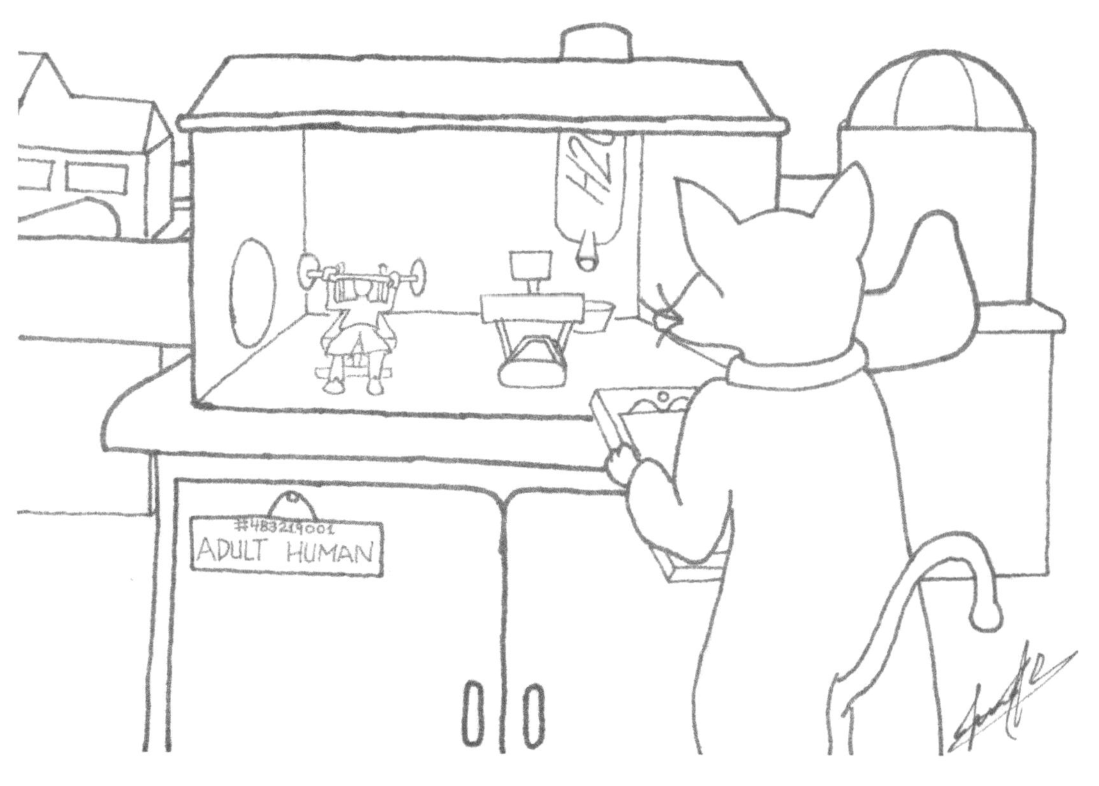

"Strange These Humans"

Because in a world where twenty-four-hour fitness facilities sprout up like an uncontrollable infection, we're still struggling with obesity.

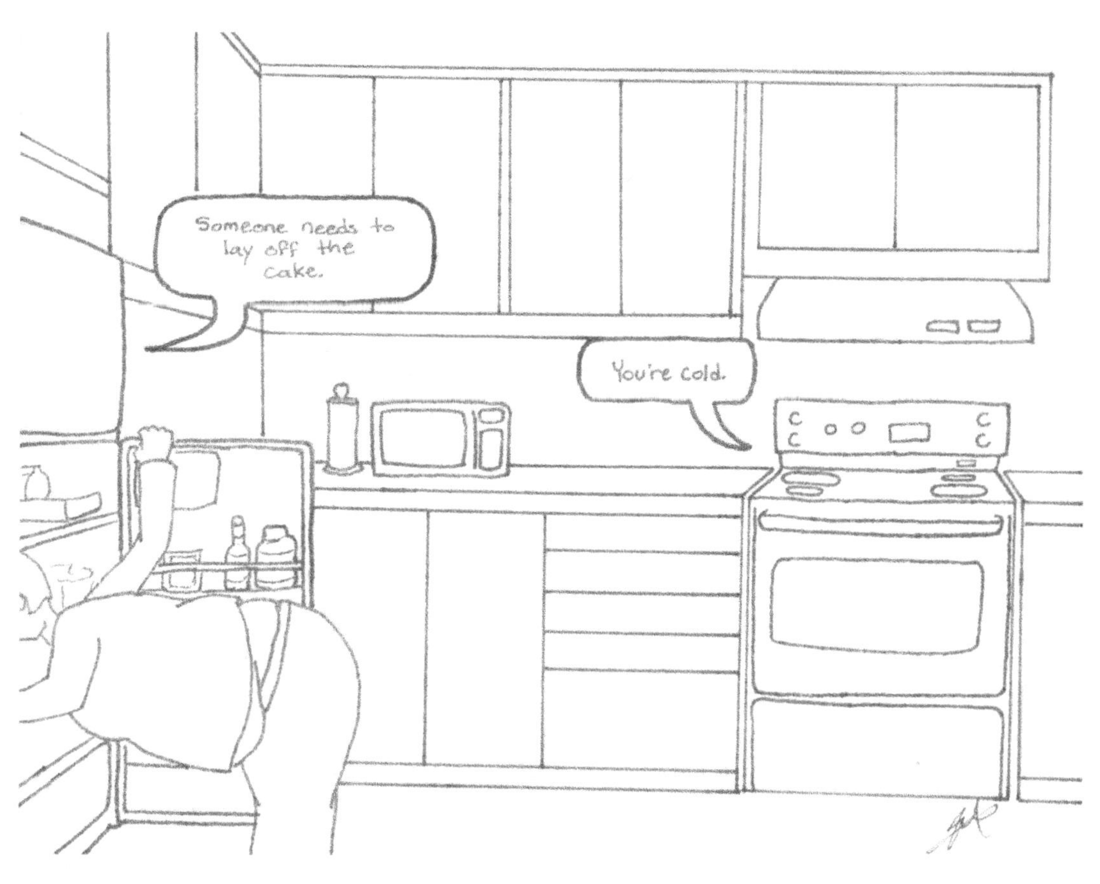

"Diet And Exercise"

And in a world where minimal effort is required to complete a task, we still feel a heavy burden.

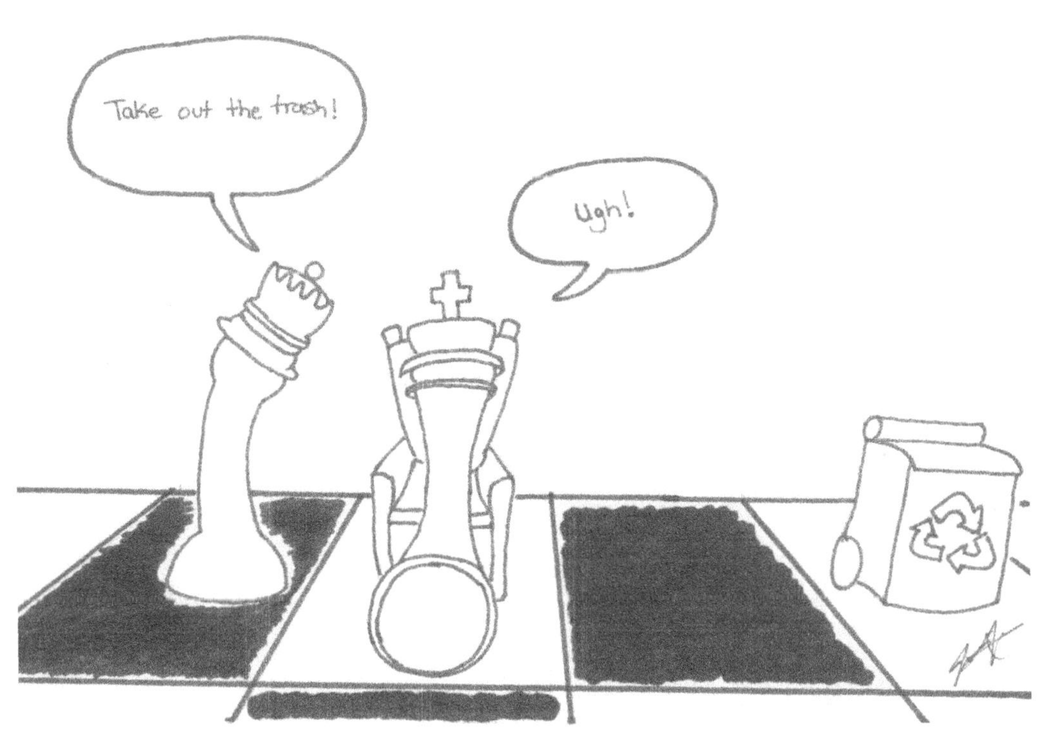

"Ruling Pains"

And in a world where honesty can alleviate stress, we still find dishonesty rewarding.

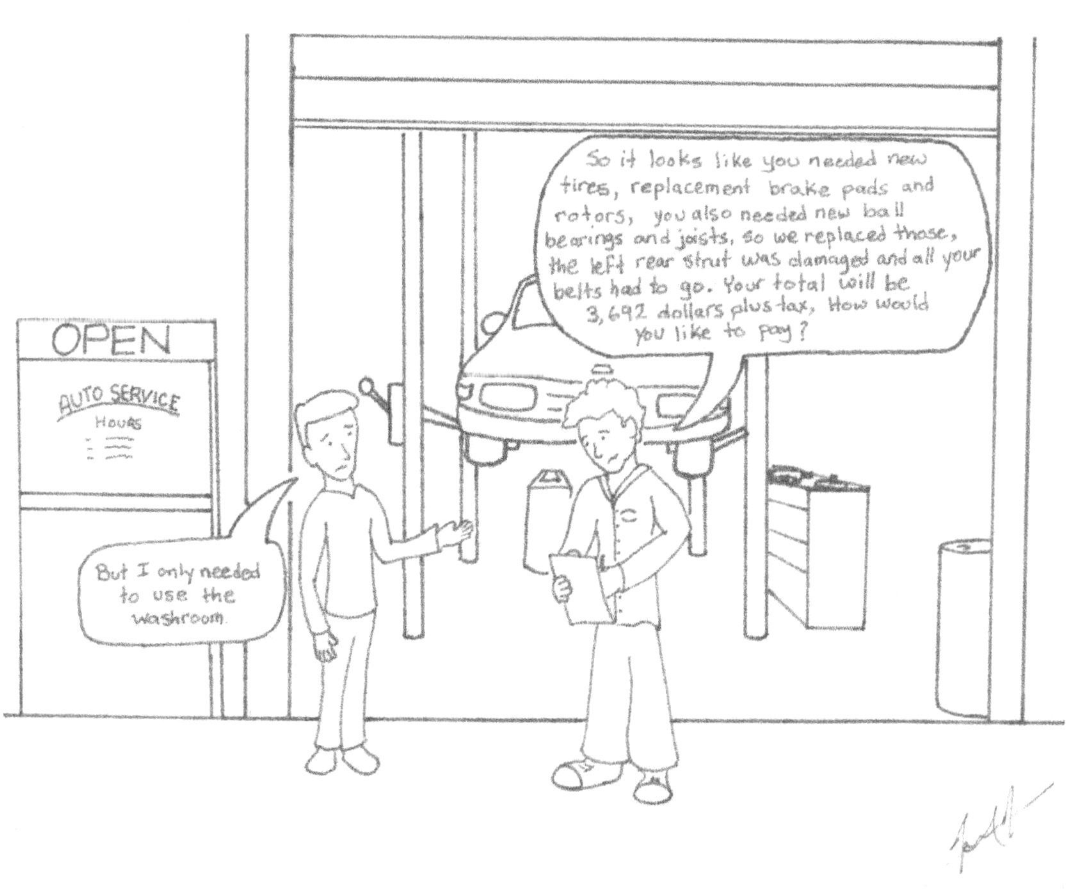

"For Paying Costumers Only"

And in a world where we have copious amounts of resources at our disposal, self-importance is still valued more than helping our fellow man.

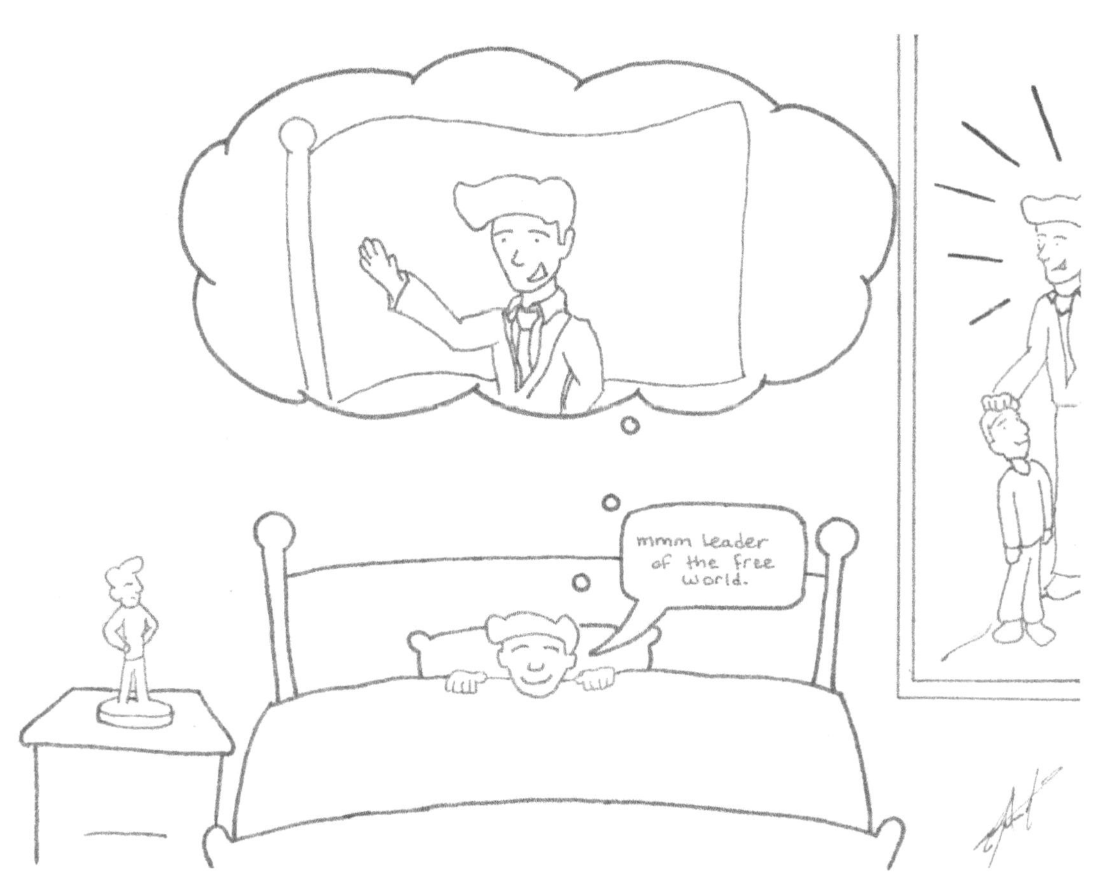

"Proud To Be"

And in a world where beauty is all around us, we choose to remain distracted.

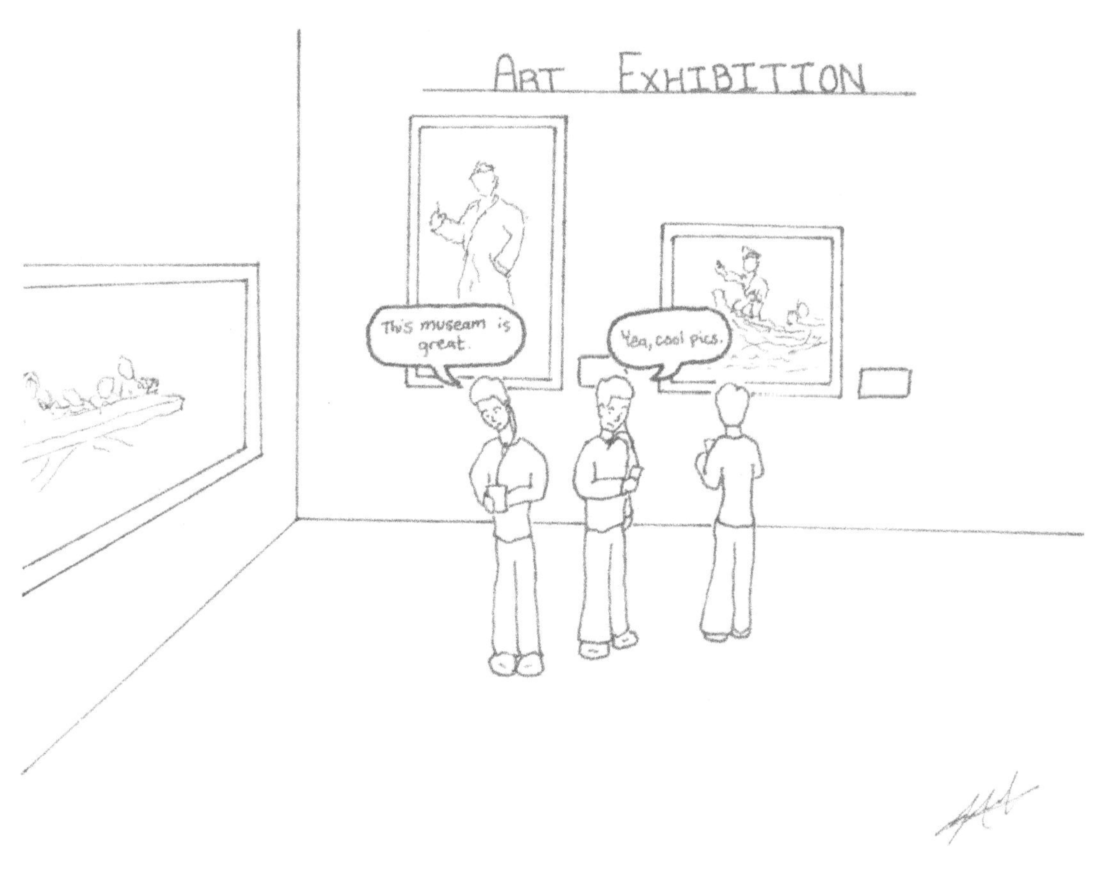

"A Distracted Generation"

And in a world where chivalry is yearned for, we choose to be douche-bags.

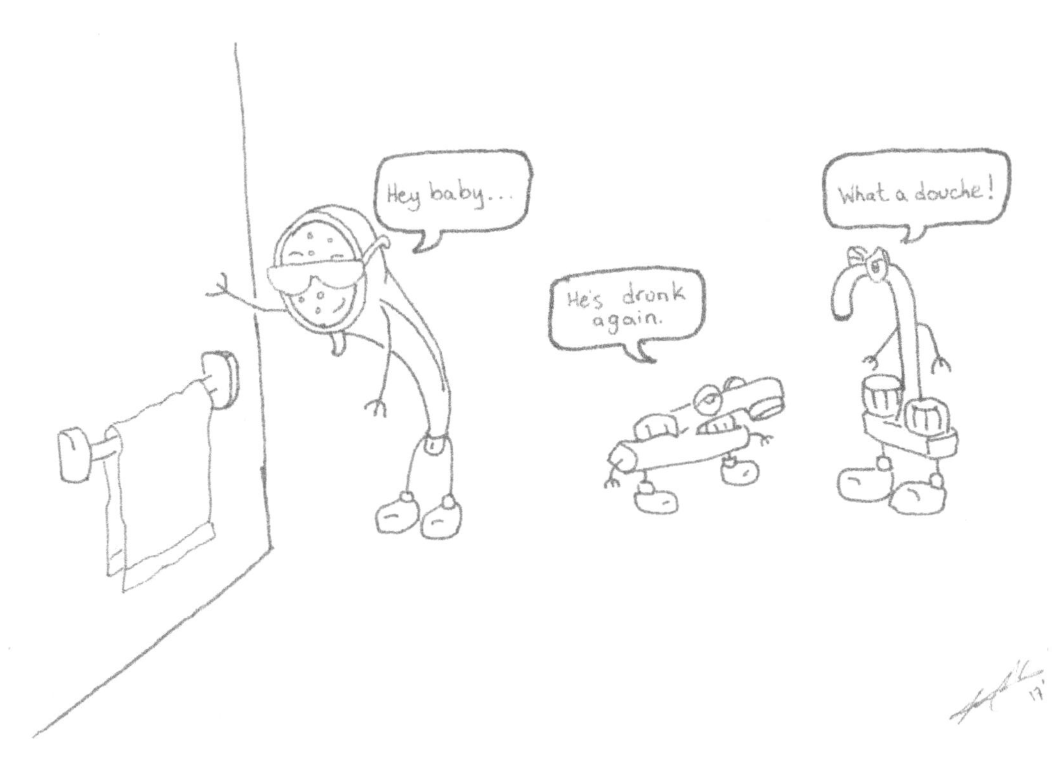

"What A Douche!"

And instead of living the dream that we were promised when we grew up, finished school and found a job, we're left stuck in a routine that we can't seem to break out of.

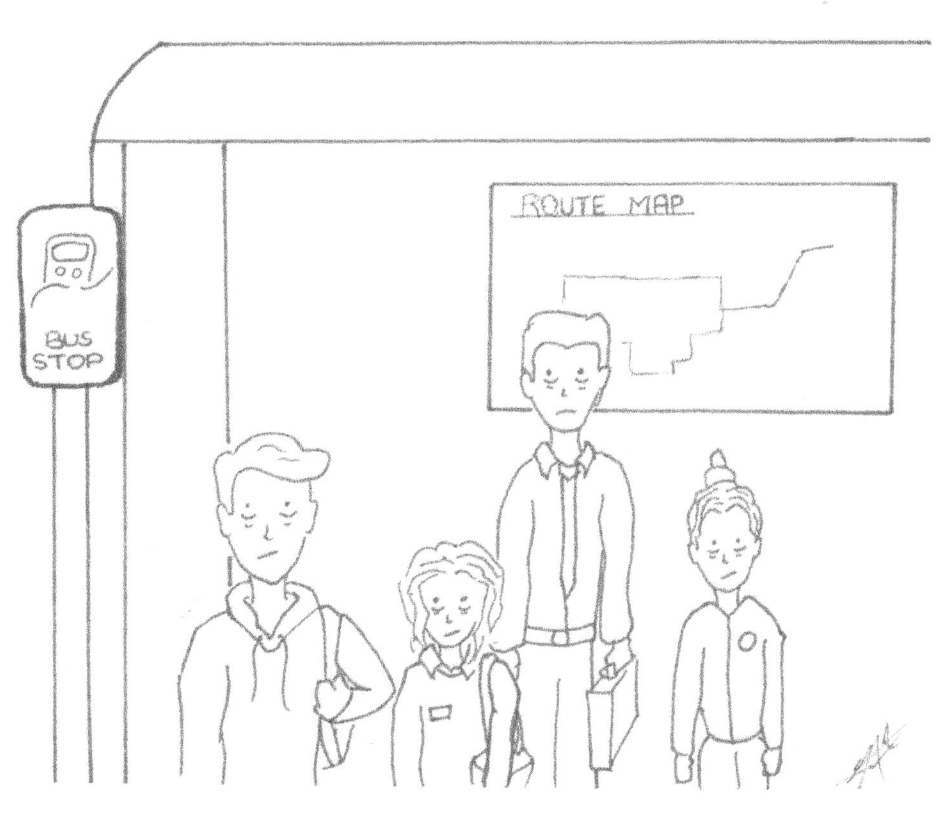

"The Canadian Dream"

Whether it's because of financial strains.

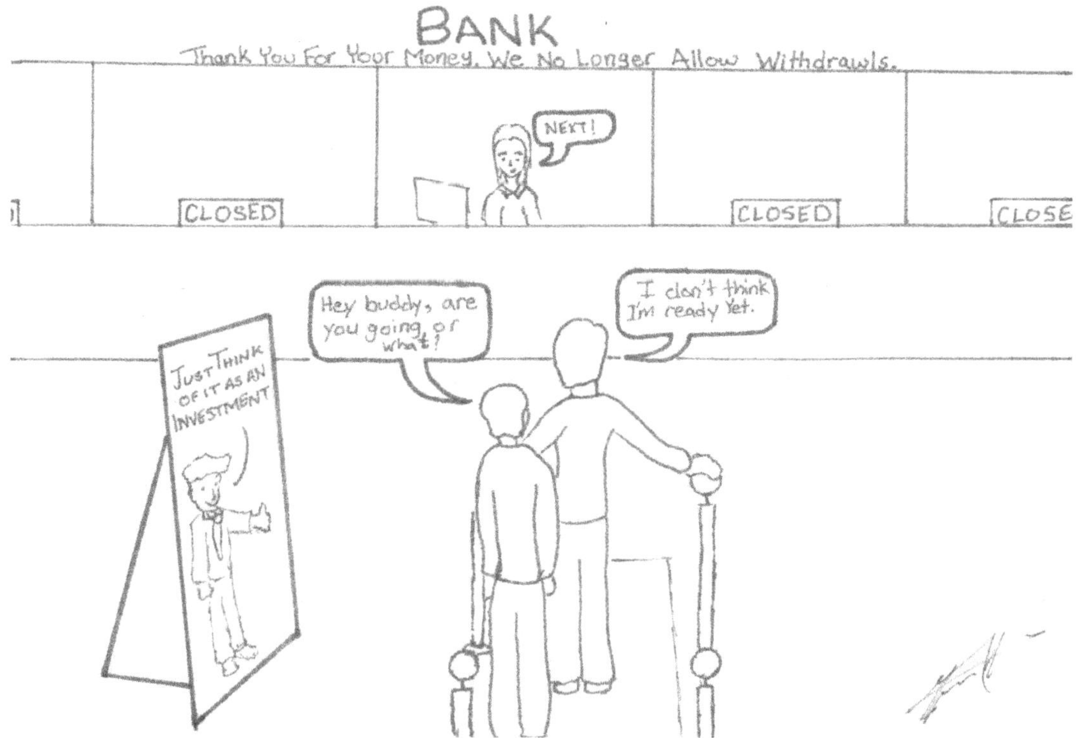
NATIONAL BANK
Thank You For Your Money. We No Longer Allow Withdrawls.
NEXT!
CLOSED
CLOSED
CLOSE
JUST THINK OF IT AS AN INVESTMENT
Hey buddy, are you going or what?
I don't think I'm ready Yet.

"Pay Day"

Ridiculous contracts and clauses.

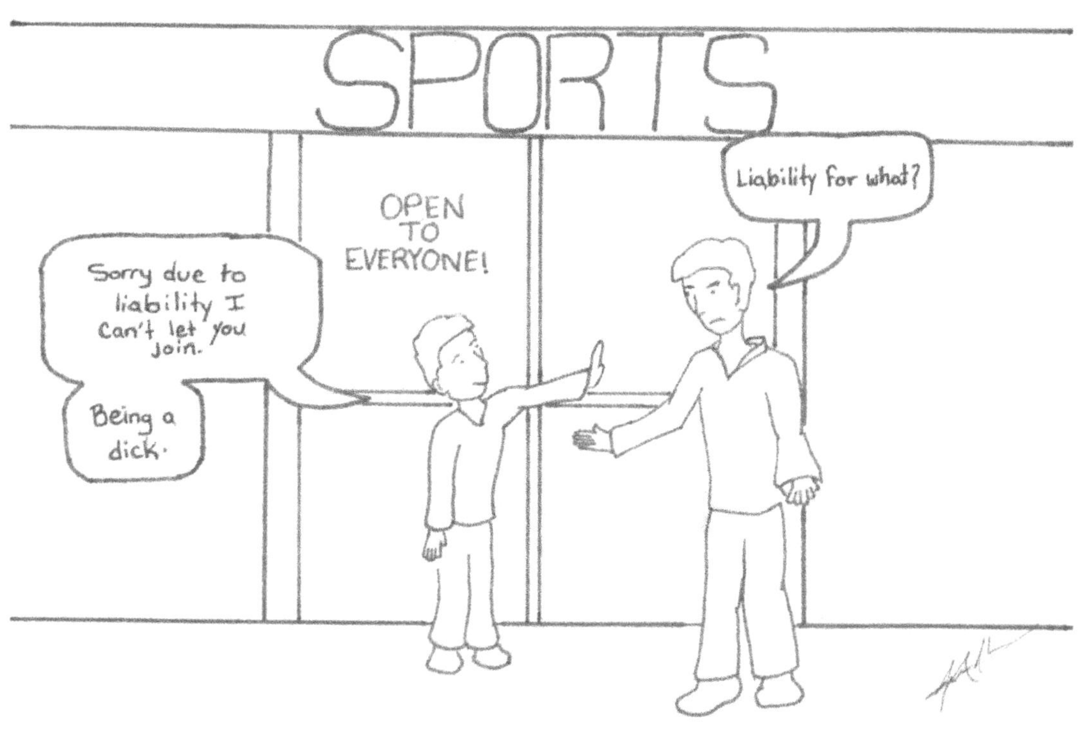

"Insurance and Liability Clause"

Or our inability to ignore the nonsense that bombards us on a daily basis.

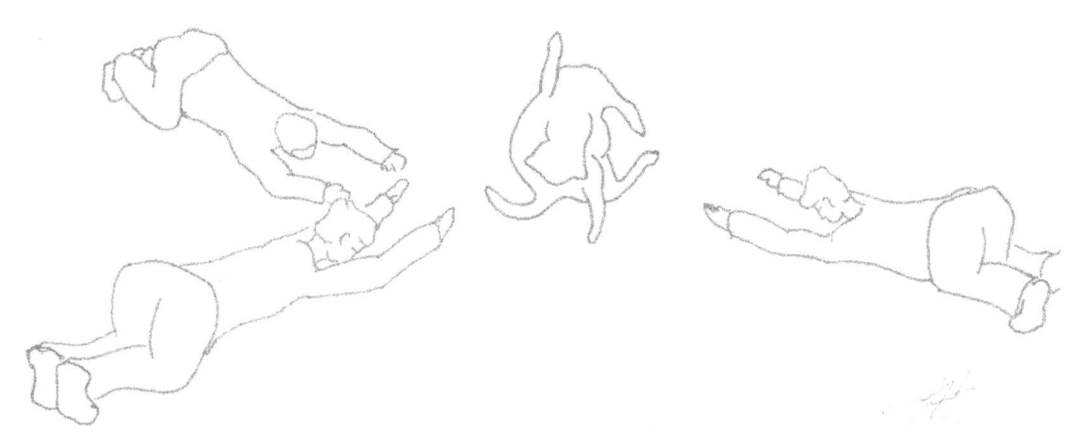

"History Repeats Itself"

And to add to the insanity that plagues humanity.

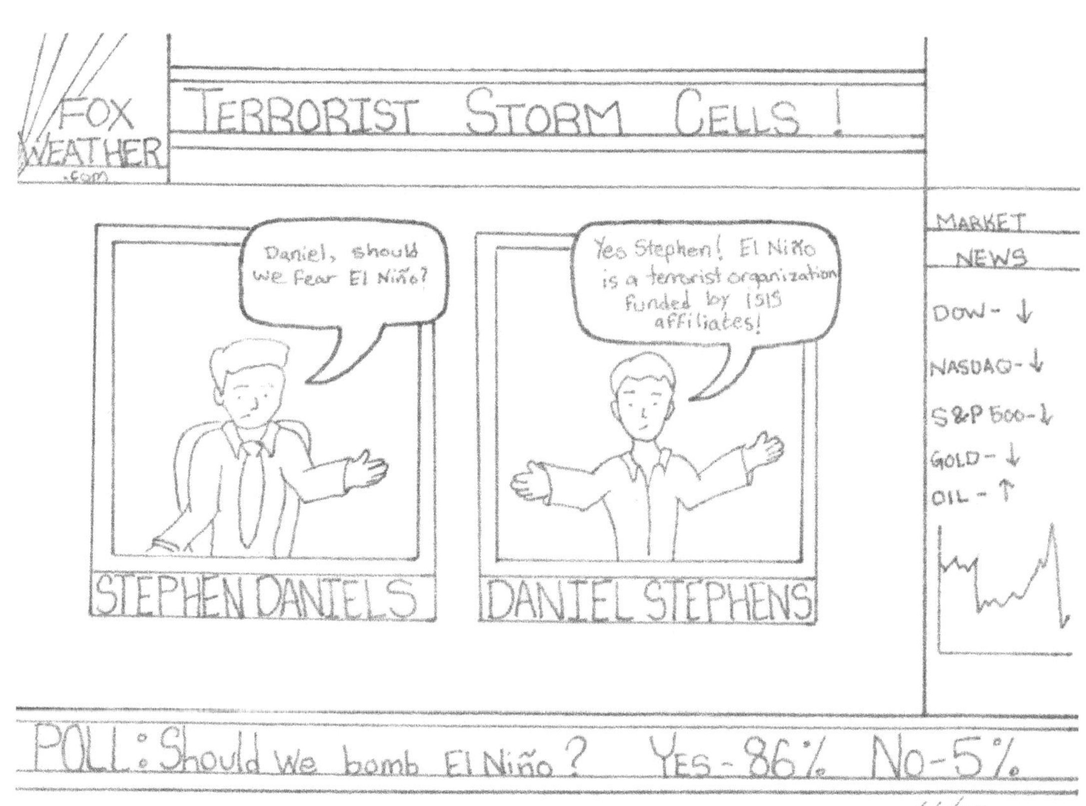
FOX WEATHER .com
TERRORIST STORM CELLS!
Daniel, should we fear El Niño?
Yes Stephen! El Niño is a terrorist organization funded by ISIS affiliates!
STEPHEN DANIELS
DANIEL STEPHENS
MARKET NEWS
DOW- ↓
NASDAQ- ↓
S&P 500- ↓
GOLD- ↓
OIL- ↑
POLL: Should we bomb El Niño? YES-86% No-5%

"El Niño

We're knowingly choosing to destroy the one thing that gives us life.

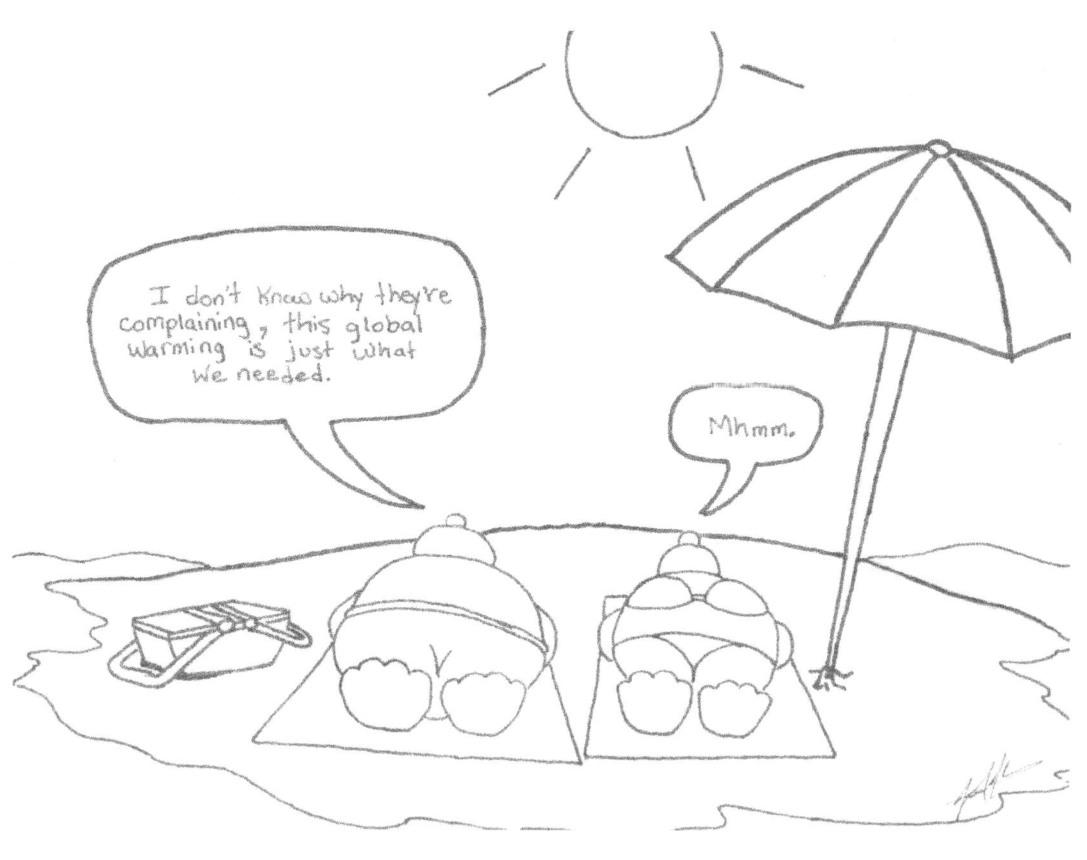

"The Ice Capps Are Melting"

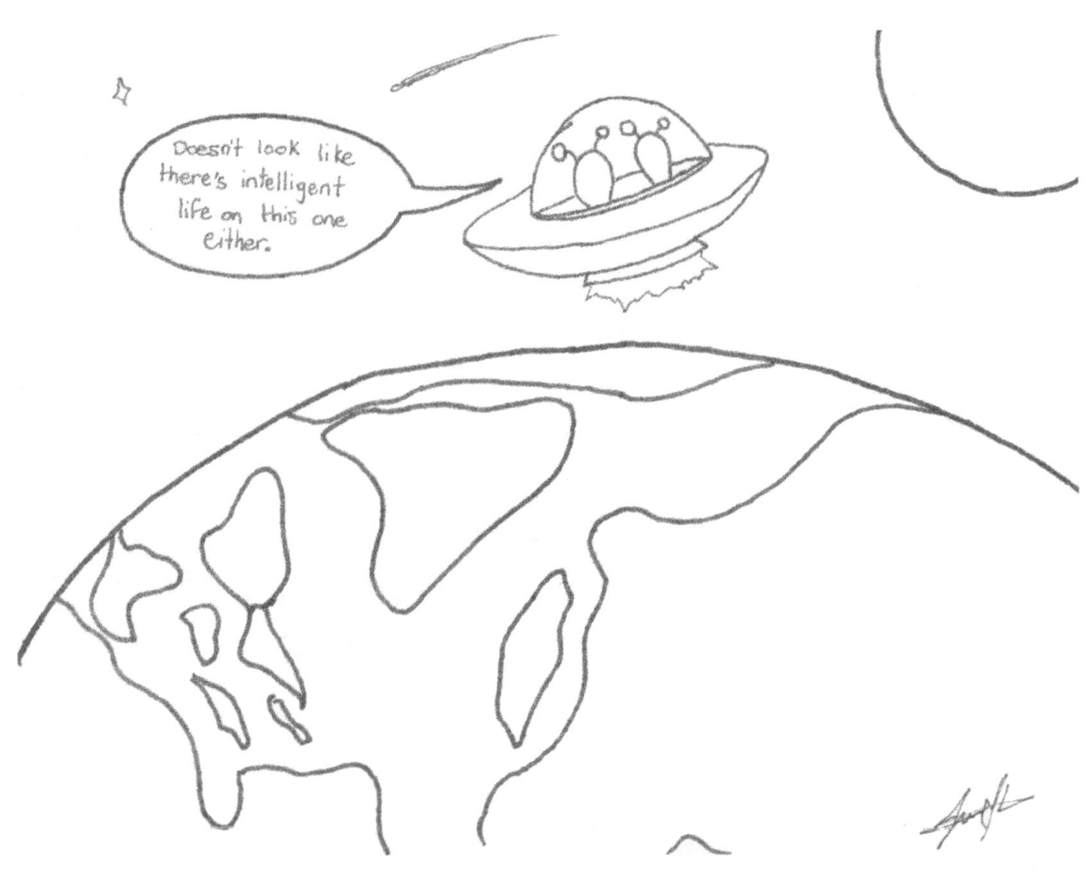

"The Search Continues"

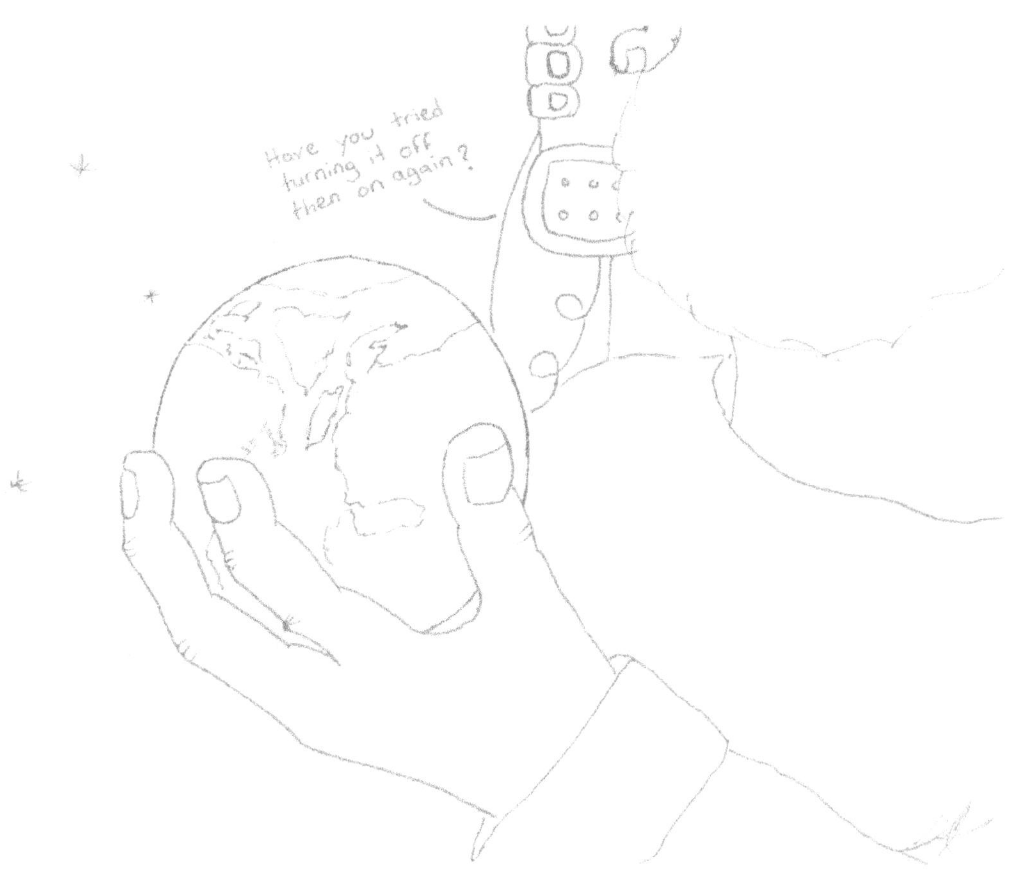

"Technical Support"

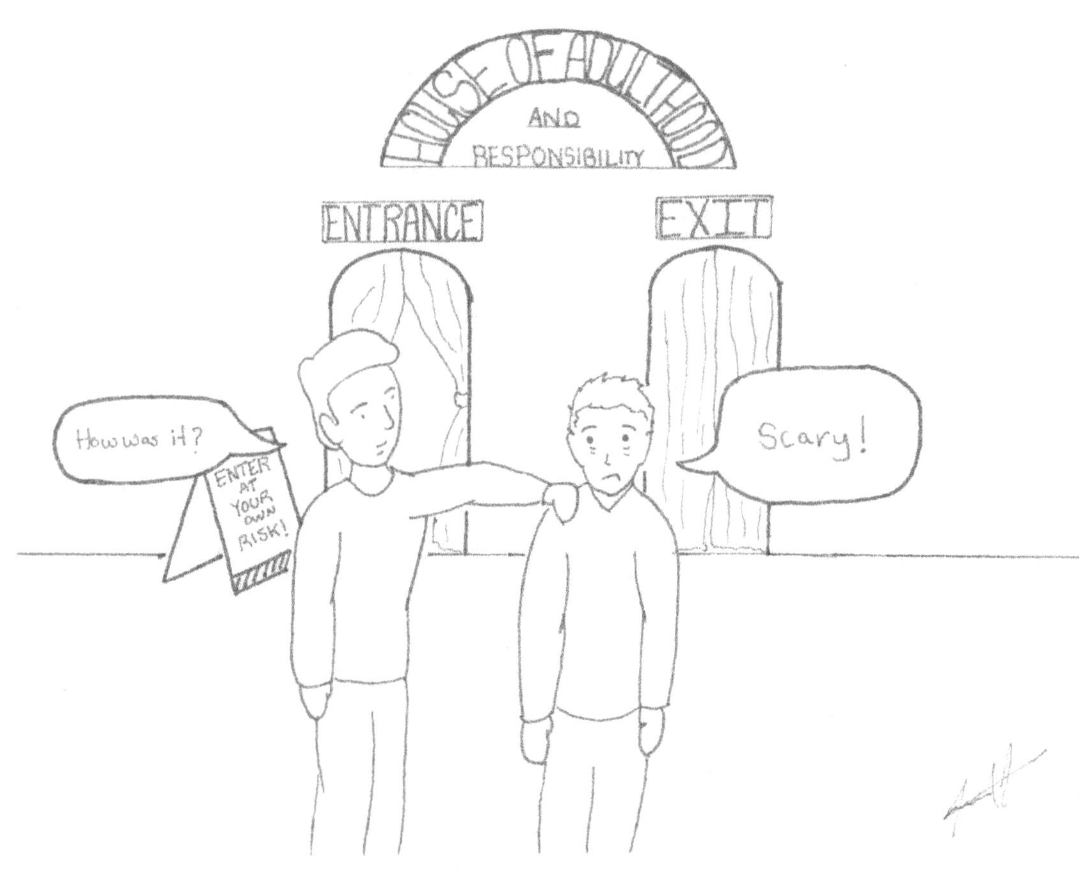
HOUSE OF ADULTHOOD
AND
RESPONSIBILITY
ENTRANCE
EXIT
How was it?
ENTER AT YOUR OWN RISK!
Scary!

"The Circus"

www.ingramcontent.com/pod-product-compliance
Lightning Source LLC
Chambersburg PA
CBHW080526030726
47592CB00012B/3488

* 9 7 8 1 7 7 5 0 7 4 5 2 6 *